"Carol has faithfully laid down her life for the gospel. And now, God has asked her to lay down her most precious treasure — her only son. Today, Carol has come away from the altar gloriously transformed . . . so will you."

— KATHY TROCCOLI, author, speaker, recording artist

"For all those experiencing Job's dark day in the present, and for all whose day is yet to come, this book points the way to the dawn of a new day."

— JILL BRISCOE, speaker, author of *A Little Pot of Oil*

"If I were to read only one book this year, it would be *When I Lay My Issac Down*. This honest, heart-wrenching story caused me to look deep within and say to God, 'Yes, I am willing to give up what I love to You who loves me more.'"

— LINDA DILLOW, author of *Calm My Anxious Heart* and *Intimacy Ignited*

"Carol Kent has poured her heart onto these pages, sharing her tragic and triumphant journey with breathtaking honesty. Her compassion for others lifts this story far above a simple testimony to God's faithfulness. *When I Lay My Isaac Down* is about a believer's faith put to the ultimate test."

— LIZ CURTIS HIGGS, best-selling author of *Bad Girls of the Bible*

"What a rare treasure it is to weep, mourn, and rejoice with Carol, finding in her words the strength in Christ to let go of my 'Isaacs.' Please receive Carol's invitation to take up our crosses together, knowing that with God, the story isn't over."

— BONNIE KEEN, writer/recording artist of the song *Isaac*

"Carol consoles others with the very same comfort she has received through God's ever-present mercy. For anyone facing the unique heartbreak of having to surrender what feels like a part of yourself, this book is a must-read."

— MICHELLE MCKINNEY HAMMOND, author of *The Diva Principle*

WHEN I LAY MY ISAAC DOWN

Unshakable Faith in

Unthinkable Circumstances

CAROL KENT

NAVPRESS

Discipleship Inside Out®

Discipleship Inside Out®

NavPress is the publishing ministry of The Navigators, an international Christian organization and leader in personal spiritual development. NavPress is committed to helping people grow spiritually and enjoy lives of meaning and hope through personal and group resources that are biblically rooted, culturally relevant, and highly practical.

For a free catalog go to www.NavPress.com
or call 1.800.366.7788 in the United States or 1.800.839.4769 in Canada.

© 2004, 2013 by Carol Kent

ISBN-13: 978-1-61291-442-8

Cover design by Arvid Wallen

Scripture quotations in this publication are taken from THE MESSAGE (MSG). Copyright © 1993, 1994, 1995, 1996, 2000, 2001, 2002. Used by permission of NavPress Publishing Group. Other versions used include: the Holy Bible, New International Version® (NIV®). Copyright © 1973, 1978, 1984, 2011 by Biblica, Inc.® Used by permission of Zondervan. All rights reserved worldwide. www.zondervan.com. The "NIV" and "New International Version" are trademarks registered in the United States Patent and Trademark Office by Biblica, Inc.®; the New American Standard Bible (NASB), © The Lockman Foundation 1960, 1962, 1963, 1968, 1971, 1972, 1973, 1975, 1977, 1995; The Living Bible (TLB). Copyright © 1971, used by permission of Tyndale House Publishers, Inc., Wheaton, IL 60189, all rights reserved; the Amplified New Testament (AMP), © The Lockman Foundation 1954, 1958; and the Holy Bible, New Living Translation (NLT). Copyright © 1996. Used by permission of Tyndale House Publishers, Inc., Wheaton, Illinois 60189. All rights reserved.

Kent, Carol, 1947-
    When I lay my Isaac down : unshakable faith in unthinkable circumstances / Carol Kent.-- 1st ed.
        p. cm.
    Includes bibliographical references.
    ISBN 1-57683-474-3
    1. Suffering--Religious aspects--Christianity. 2. Sacrifice--Christianity. 3. Kent, Carol, 1947- 4. Kent, Jason Paul. 5. Parent and child--Religious aspects--Christianity. 6. Murder--Religious aspects--Christianity. I. Title.
    BV4909.K46 2004
    248.8'6--dc22
                                        2004004140

Printed in the United States of America

1 2 3 4 5 6 7 8 / 18 17 16 15 13

DEDICATION

This book is dedicated to our

"Stretcher Bearers"

*and to all of you who take the time
to respond to the needs of others
by answering the question,
"How can I help with tangible encouragement?"*

*Our "Stretcher Bearers" became the
hands and feet of Jesus to us
when we ran out of resources.*

*You have modeled a lifestyle of giving
that has forever changed our lives.*

*Please hold Gene and me accountable
for "finishing well."*

CONTENTS

Circumstances may appear to wreck
our lives and God's plans,
but God is not helpless among the ruins.

— ERIC LIDDELL, OLYMPIAN

DOES *L*IFE GET ANY BETTER THAN *THIS?*

IT WAS AN IDYLLIC FALL DAY. OUR MICHIGAN TREES HAD turned from their magnificent summer greens to a panoramic pallet of golden yellows, burnished oranges, russet browns, and deep reds. My husband, Gene, and I walked hand in hand along the glorious two-mile stretch of sidewalk beside the St. Clair River. The sun rose high in the azure sky, producing a reflection on the river that lived up to the advertisements in local Chamber of Commerce brochures. The complete tranquility of that moment is frozen in my memory.

We paused along the walkway, inhaling the fresh, crisp air, and talked about all of the good things that had been happening in our lives. Our son, J.P., had graduated from the U.S. Naval Academy a couple of years earlier, and we recounted the pride and joy we experienced on his graduation day in Annapolis, Maryland. He was an officer in the navy with a bright future, and he had married a delightful young woman just the year before. With his marriage to April, he also became a devoted stepfather to her precious young daughters, Chelsea and Hannah. We adored our granddaughters and looked forward to watching this young family thrive. Gene's business was flourishing. My speaking and writing career had exploded with opportunities for international travel and stimulating variety. We were young empty nesters entering what had all of the potential of becoming the best season of our lives.

After naming our blessings with grateful hearts, I looked up at my husband and said, "Does life get any better than *this?*" We finished the walk with our arms encircled around each other's waists, never dreaming that in less than two weeks, everything about our future would change.

This book is the story of two parents who received the devastating news that their remarkable son, a young lieutenant in the Navy, had committed a crime so unthinkable it was impossible to believe. For a long time I could not talk about my pain, and I could not write publicly about what I was feeling. There are some tragedies that are too big for a heart to hold, and they defy any description that makes sense. Time weaves its way through the shock, the hurt, and the inexpressible feelings, and one day you discover that in the process of daily survival, you have instinctively made decisions (good and bad), defined your theology, formed an opinion about God, and determined that you will either curl up and die emotionally or you will choose life.

The terrifying but truthful fact is that, in choosing life, you realize it will never match the kind of life that was in your carefully thought-out plan for your future. It will force you to view the people around you differently. The brokenness will challenge you to new levels of personal compassion. It will melt your pride, diminish the importance of your carefully designed agenda, and it has the potential to develop an unshakable faith that defies rationality. It is my prayer that *When I Lay My Isaac Down* will forever change your view of personal challenges.

Part of this book will examine a man named Abraham. He had a son. I have a son. His son had done nothing wrong. My son committed murder. This book is not about the sons. It is about people who make heart sacrifices while living in the midst of uncertain circumstances in a world where many things make no earthly sense. Abraham made choices that teach us how to live with purpose in an imperfect world. Other Bible characters did too.

There are times in life when all of us are called upon to make heart sacrifices. Some of those sacrifices are things we choose because of a cause we believe in or a desired end that makes our decision worthwhile. However, most of us will face an "Isaac experience," when a crisis is thrust into our lives without warning and without survival instructions. Our "Isaacs" are the heart sacrifices we make when we choose to relinquish control and honor God with our choices even when all seems lost. We have to decide if we will let go of our control over a person, situation, or event, or if we will hang on for dear life and refuse to relinquish something we cherish.

As much as I don't like the process, I am learning that the cup of sorrow can also be the cup of joy. If you choose to embrace the principles outlined in this book, I pray that you will be infused with a fresh perspective on how to be authentic, courageous, and steadfast as you discover the hidden power in heart sacrifices. All of us have circumstances that produce varying degrees of personal loss and devastation. Will we maintain our grip on hope in the process of defeat? Will we live our lives with passion and purpose even if, in this lifetime, we are not permitted to have an answer to why something has happened? Will we choose unshakable faith, or will we give up on God? I believe God's great invitation is to engage us in the process of discovering the power of choosing faith when that decision makes no sense. There is hidden power in our unthinkable circumstances.

Four years have come and gone since I asked my husband the question, "Does life get any better than *this?*" It's been the hardest and most painful four years of my life, but what I have learned about authentic faith and about what really matters in life doesn't get much better than this. In the middle of laying our Isaacs down, we are not alone. Anne Lamott describes the awareness of His presence in the middle of desperate circumstances:

> After a while, as I lay there, I became aware of someone with me, hunkered down in the corner, and I just assumed it was my father, whose presence I had felt over the years when I was frightened and alone. The feeling was so strong that I actually turned on the light for a moment to make sure no one was there — of course, there wasn't. But after a while, in the dark again, I knew beyond any doubt that it was Jesus. . . . I felt him just sitting there on his haunches in the corner of my sleeping loft, watching me with patience and love.[1]

This has been my most important discovery, and it is my prayer for you as you read this book. When God seems the most absent, He is the most present. He is in the middle of your circumstances whether or not you have recognized Him.

Because it's so hard to think clearly when the unthinkable happens, I offer you some questions to reflect on at the end of each chapter. You may find it helpful to write your thoughts in a journal or talk about them with a friend or in a small group. Or, if you're the friend of the person who's facing the unthinkable, you may find these questions useful as you seek to offer support.

As you embrace God's enduring, unconditional love, I pray that you will discover an unshakable faith that defies description welling up and infusing your soul with courage.

※ ※ ※

Ten years have passed since this book was originally written, and much has happened since the story recorded on these pages took place. This updated and revised edition of the book has a second epilogue that will bring you up to date on our adventure in faith.

$\mathcal{A}$N UNEXPECTED JOURNEY

The Power *of* Unthinkable Circumstances

There are moments when God makes utter and complete sense to us, and then suddenly, life changes and he seems a foreign remnant of a childhood force-fed faith. . . . "[Lord,] give us eyes to see your coming and going, ears to hear your voice and your silence, hands to hold your presence and your absence, and faith to trust your unchanging nature in all seasons."
—ELISA MORGAN

THE PHONE RANG IN THE MIDDLE OF THE NIGHT. I SQUINTED in the direction of the alarm clock as Gene reached for the receiver. It was 12:35 A.M. Who would be calling at this hour? Listening to my husband, I instantly knew he was receiving dreadful news.

Gene pulled the receiver back and haltingly choked out the words. "J.P. has been arrested."

I was dumbfounded. What illegal act could my son possibly have done that would have resulted in an arrest? My husband continued speaking with tears spilling down his cheeks. "He's been arrested for the first-degree murder of Douglas Miller Jr."

My feet hit the floor as I tried to get out of bed, but my legs were incapable of holding my weight. I slumped to all fours. Nausea swept over me. I began crawling toward the bathroom where I could throw up, but everything was in slow motion. I had never before experienced shock. No strength. Wave after wave of nausea. Dizziness. I had to remind myself to breathe.

Thoughts began swirling in my head. *This must be a mistake. Or a cruel joke. Perhaps it's a case of mistaken identity. Maybe I'm living inside a horrific dream. Surely this news is not true. Someone is playing a perverse game. My son is not capable of taking the life of another human being, much less a premeditated act of such violence. This is not happening. My son is a dynamic Christian. He's a graduate of the United States Naval Academy. He defends American citizens; he doesn't destroy them. I will go back to sleep and wake up in reality.*

Our daughter-in-law, April, was still on the phone and through hysterical sobs of her own, she verified that she had just received a call from Jason at a jail in downtown Orlando, Florida, and he had been arrested for the murder of her ex-husband. Gene tried to calm her while simultaneously dealing with his own raw emotions. We were filled with incredulous thoughts. *How? Why? What really happened? What was Jason doing in Orlando, a six-and-a-half-hour drive from his home in Panama City? Was it an accident? Was it self-defense?*

The next few hours were a blur of tears, panic, fear, and erratic, meaningless activity. It was after 1:00 A.M. when Gene finished the conversation with April. Still on my haunches on the floor, I called the Orlando jail to see if anyone named Jason Kent had been brought to the facility. The woman on the end of the phone line was rude and irritated; her speech was slurred. "Lady, we ain't got nobody by that name, Jason Kent, in here. Your son ain't here."

For a few brief moments hope returned. It *was* a mistake. Our son had *not* been arrested. Jason was okay and we would be okay. But within an hour, another call confirmed our worst fears. Jason Paul Kent, our only child, son of my womb, was locked up at the Thirty-Third Street facility in Orlando. And he was being held without bond on the worst felony charge possible — first-degree murder.

Florida is a death-penalty state. My mind flashed to the documentary I had seen the week before, giving the blow-by-blow account of an inmate on death row. *Would my son end up in the electric chair?* I choked out a fresh sob.

As the next few hours crawled by, Gene and I held each other and wept. Two parents in the grip of a nightmare. A mom and a dad who loved their child deeply. A child who had been a joy to raise. A focused, disciplined, compassionate, dynamic, encouraging young man who wanted to live for things that mattered. A young adult who had dedicated himself to serving his God and his country through military service in the U.S. Navy. But that day the unthinkable roared into our lives. Without warning our dreams for our only child came crashing down in a thousand broken pieces. Our whole world felt shattered.

DESPERATE PARENTS

Throughout the wee hours of that morning Gene and I watched the clock as darkness slowly turned to dawn. I had always taught other people to pray when they were in trouble. It was easy to tell somebody else what to do during a crisis, but living through our own unspeakable situation was different. I am a woman who takes action. I am a researcher, a public speaker, a leader in my community. Surely there was something I could *do* to fix this horrible problem. But I didn't know where to begin.

My mind recalled a verse from the book of James:

If you don't know what you're doing, pray to the Father. He loves to help. You'll get his help, and won't be condescended to when you ask for it. Ask boldly, believingly, without a second thought. People who "worry their prayers" are like wind-whipped waves.[1]

Gene and I didn't do formal prayers that morning. We did wailing, pleading, moaning prayers. "God, please protect and comfort our son. God, please send Your angels to console the family of Douglas Miller. Please put Your arms around April, Chelsea, and Hannah (our granddaughters). God, *please* help us to know what to do and who to call. We are *desperate* for wisdom. We need You. *Please.*"

Looking back, I believe our prayers were more like "wind-whipped waves" than bold, believing prayers. We were begging God for assistance. We had never felt so needy in our lives. We alternately burst into sobs and clung to each other, followed by intermittent list making. Relatives needed to be notified and action steps had to be taken. We needed to see our son. If this had really happened, then J.P. needed his parents. He also needed an attorney. We needed the best legal counsel available and we didn't know where to go for help.

I quickly discovered that a person who is in shock cannot think beyond the moment. I could only do one thing at a time, and for the next several hours we did "the next thing" one item at a time. At sunrise Gene called the only pastor we knew in the Orlando area, Dr. Joel Hunter of Northland Community Church (where J.P. and April had first met, followed by a whirlwind romance). Gene asked Joel if he knew of any outstanding criminal defense attorneys in central Florida. Joel assured us he would call back as soon as he got the advice of people he trusted.

Our next call was to our brother-in-law and lifelong friend, Graydon Dimkoff. As a family court judge in western Michigan, we hoped that my sister Jennie's husband might be able to guide us to a resource that would lead to a competent attorney. Within an hour the pastor in Florida and the judge in Michigan returned calls to us with the identical recommendation for a criminal defense attorney. Gene and I believed this was a direct answer to prayer. Before 10:00 A.M., attorney Bill Barnett had agreed to take Jason's case.

With the assurance of legal counsel, we were also informed of the fee for this service — a sum much larger than we could have imagined. We needed to empty the savings account, cash in retirement funds, and figure out a way to give our son the best legal defense possible.

Our crisis was only hours old, and on the surface we were moving forward with decisions that were difficult, necessary, and important. But inside our souls we were curling up in the fetal position and wishing to die. I wailed, "God! This is too big for me. I cannot walk this road. Please, take me home to be with You right now. God, *please* . . . I don't know how to live through this."

But even as I uttered that prayer I knew my son needed me more now than he ever had before. He was locked up in a maximum-security jail with more than 4,000 other prisoners. We could not telephone him and had no way of knowing what his physical and mental condition was. As my thoughts hovered over all of the frightening possibilities of debilitating harm Jason faced in his current circumstances, my heart started palpitating and my breathing was labored.

As night turned to morning, I was in too much of an emotional upheaval to make the necessary calls to relatives. Gene carefully made a list of people who needed to be contacted before they got their information from a newspaper or from a stranger, and one by one he began making the calls. First, he asked Graydon and Jennie to tell my parents in person. They live in the same town on the other side of Michigan from where we live. We feared that one or both of Jason's grandparents might have heart attacks when they received the news. J.P. is the oldest grandchild in the family and deeply loved and respected by my mother and dad.

Following my sister and brother-in-law's visit to their home with the devastating news, Mom and Dad called us. The exact wording of our conversation is a blur, but one thing about that call stands out: We sobbed together over the phone. Before the conversation was concluded, my parents assured me of their love for us and for J.P., and then my father prayed for all of us. Dad is a semiretired preacher and his deep, resonant, pastoral voice was a comfort to my desperate and weary soul.

Jennie called later that morning, and once again I experienced the "fellowship of tears" with one of my four precious sisters. We are the oldest of our parents' six children, and even though I'm four years older than Jennie, our deep heart connection has long caused us to refer to ourselves as "twins born four years apart." When I picked up the receiver, Jennie's voice was such a comfort to me. Our children were as close as siblings, and Jennie loved Jason deeply.

"Oh, Jen," I stammered, "I don't know how to fix this. I don't know what to do next. I don't know where to go for help. I don't know how to help my boy."

I could hear her labored breathing between sobs as we held each other as closely as the telephone would allow.

Gene's mom called and cried with us over the phone too. Gene had asked his brother, David, to break the news to his mother and her husband, Bruce. Bruce has been Gene's stepfather for over three decades, and J.P. spent a lot of time with this set of grandparents during his growing-up years. He was their pride and joy, and they were in deep agony over this shocking report.

Gene's father is a man of few words, and after David broke the news to him, he called us and struggled through an emotional response. He ended the call by saying, "I love you, son." I could see tears in Gene's eyes as he hung up the phone.

When it rang again, my best friend from high school, Jan Fleck, was on the line. Jan and I have known each other since we were fourteen years old and remain close friends to this day. Both of us lead busy lives and we aren't in contact weekly, but she seems to have a "sixth sense" when I have a need for prayer. This time we hadn't communicated with each other for a couple of months and when I picked up the phone, she asked immediately, "How are you?"

"Not very well," I sputtered. "How did you know to call me *today?* J.P. has been arrested for first-degree murder." She was not prepared to hear those shocking words, but she knew God had prompted her to call me. We were two redheads who had encouraged each other spiritually for several decades — kindred-heart sisters who prayed for each other regularly. She loved my son. I don't remember the rest of the conversation, but that morning I felt the power of knowing that a friend was weeping with me. I knew I was not alone.

Later that day, Dr. Joel Hunter became Jason's first visitor at the Orange County Jail. Immediately afterward Pastor Joel called us and said that our son was a broken young man, still stunned by the ramifications of his actions. Joel went on to say that they had gripped each other's hands tightly and he had prayed with J.P.

Intermittently throughout that interminable day, denial kicked in and I once again believed I was living inside a grotesque nightmare. Several hours later, however, a collect phone call brought all denial to a stunned halt.

"Mom and Dad?" Our son's voice was soft, and I sensed his broken and crushed spirit.

"J.P., are you okay?" we asked, almost simultaneously. We were so grateful to hear his voice.

"I'm all right." I sensed my son's feeling of being unworthy to voice any concern for himself and his circumstances in light of what had transpired the day before.

For at least a full minute there were no words — just shared tears between a father, a mother, and their only child.

"J.P., we love you and we are here for you," I assured him through intense emotions. "We will always love you. You are not alone."

Gene added, "We've hired an attorney for you who has been highly recommended to us."

"Thank you, Mom and Dad."

We prayed over the phone for J.P.'s safety, for his mental and emotional state, for the family of Douglas Miller Jr., for wisdom to know what actions to take, and for God to help us. The call was terminated abruptly by the cutoff of the digitized telephone system at the jail that regulates the length of all inmates' calls.

LIVING *on the* EDGE *of* REALITY

The next day I had a long-awaited appointment for my annual gynecological exam. I vacillated about whether or not to go. I was getting nothing done at home. Only a handful of people knew about our circumstances, and I needed to have a prescription filled. I decided to go.

The waiting room at the doctor's office was filled with women and children who were happily laughing and interacting with each other. A very pregnant mother tried to balance a two-year-old on her lap, and she flashed a smile in my direction. Another woman was paying her bill at the counter. Others were watching a soap opera on the television in the waiting area.

I felt like I was sitting on the edge of the real world, but the feeling was otherworldly — like I was an observer, not a participant, in what was going on around me. Countless thoughts somersaulted wildly in my mind. *How can the people in this room act so normal when my entire life is falling apart? I wonder if they can see the agony on my face when they look at me. I pray that none of my friends walk through the entrance, because I will fall apart if I have to face them. I'm sure God doesn't love me, and I don't think I love Him either. I hate what I'm experiencing. My son used to be as adorable as the two-year-old on that mommy's lap. How does a child go from that level of innocence to taking the life of someone else? I shouldn't be here. I should have stayed at home.*

Suddenly my name was called and I was ushered into the examining room. I quickly donned the paper gown women wear for the dreaded pap smear. I was sitting at the end of the examining table when the nurse reappeared. "Are you ready for the doctor?" Before I could answer, she spoke again: "Are you okay?" I burst into tears. I *wasn't* okay. I wasn't even *close* to being okay, but it felt good to be near a compassionate person, even though the nurse didn't know the real reason behind my tears. She walked over to the table and put an affirming hand on my shoulder. Leaning closer, she said, "The exam won't be that painful."

The moment suddenly felt even more surreal and bizarre. For the first time in forty-eight hours I laughed out loud. It was only one of many times when "black humor" would strike me at the oddest moments. The nurse thought my anxiety was induced by my fear of the gynecological exam. If she only knew the *real* source of my distress! I felt deep sadness for my son and for the family of the son who was now dead. I felt betrayed by God and helpless to change anything. Life could never be the same again — and I had been in this strange, distorted facsimile of reality for only two days.

Gene began to chronicle the devastation in his journal.

October 25 — We received the news that J.P. was arrested. Cried. Found an attorney.

October 26 — Coped poorly. Cried. I am so afraid for my son.

October 27 — Carol and I go through the motions of being alive, but inside we are dying.

In my own journal the next day, I wrote:

Laurie (my assistant) brought a blood pressure cuff to the house, and Gene and I took our blood pressure readings. For the third time this week mine was higher than it normally is. I suddenly blurted out, "I am the mother of a murderer." My sobs could not be stifled.

The love poured out from family and friends is beyond description.

Gene and I hold each other, weep, and feel each other's pain during unusual moments each day. When one is strong, it seems the other is weak.

The phone does not stop ringing.

WRESTLING *with the* ENEMY

Jason Kent loved people, and he was committed to Christ. He had a stellar record in high school, lettered in sports, and was president of the National Honor Society. In addition to volunteering with Habitat for Humanity, he mentored younger students, and he gave blood every time the Red Cross was in need. He earned a black belt in karate and was a leader in his church youth group. He was a typical teenager and young adult, but he was easy to raise. He never caused us to have serious concerns regarding any inappropriate behavior: he did not get caught up in drugs, alcohol, or hanging out with "the wrong crowd." As a student in the United States Naval Academy at Annapolis, Maryland, he studied hard and earned good grades. He was a disciplined person, physically and mentally. He joined the sailing team and set his sights on serving his country as a Navy SEAL.

If the allegations of what happened on October 24, 1999, were true, then we instinctively assumed that our son had snapped — emotionally, mentally, and spiritually. How could it be that *our son* had stooped to this act of violence? For him to get to the place of being able to pull the trigger and kill a man, something was going on in his head that Gene and I could not see. We were desperately sad we did not see warning signs that might have allowed us to intervene. We didn't know what had happened inside our son's brain, but we knew that there was nothing about his crime that was justifiable.

My mind flashed to the invisible world, and I could envision Satan laughing with a cadre of demons. They were having fun, and in between cackles several of them looked in my direction as the leader pointed at me and said, "Let's wipe her out spiritually and emotionally. Let's put a guilt trip on that mother that will make her give up on God. We'll put such financial and personal stress in the lives of the Kents that they'll give up on their faith." I could hear the creatures jeering in the background. And I sobbed.

The Enemy quickly seized the opportune moment and delivered his lies to my heart. In my wounded state of mind, all of the untruths were entirely believable.

Lie #1: I must have done something wrong as a parent or this wouldn't have happened.

Lie #2: If I had read my Bible more consistently, prayed more intensely, and stayed closer to God, I could have prevented this terrible thing from taking place.

Lie #3:   If I had been less busy, I could have fixed the problem before
         it got out of hand.

Lie #4:   If I were a more perfect Christian, God would protect my
         family and me from such hurtful circumstances.

As I struggled to make it through the next several hours, the lies hovered over my mind like vultures as the Enemy tried to control my emotions. Feeling panic, shame, and guilt, I went from window to window and closed the blinds. I envisioned reporters at the door with a multitude of questions that my husband and I couldn't answer.

One of many desperate scribblings in my journal during that time reflects my anguish:

> When your only offspring commits a murder, you can't think of your-
> self as "a good parent." Will Gene and I ever stop wondering what we
> could have done differently in our parenting that would have prohibi-
> ted our son from taking the life of another human being? We did the
> best we knew how to do. Obviously, it wasn't good enough. Does that
> mean we were bad parents? Who knows? Definitely, we should have
> been better parents.

While I was feeling lost at sea in a tidal wave of fear and despair, Gene found a life preserver by going to the Word of God seeking wisdom and solace. In his journal he wrote about the day he picked up his Bible for the first time since the appalling news smashed our world:

> I started reading where I had left off last week. I'm in Genesis 28
> where Jacob falls into a dream and sees a ladder. The bottom of the
> ladder is resting on earth, but the top reaches to heaven and God's
> angels are going up and down on the ladder. Jacob awakens, more
> alert than he's ever been, and he realizes, perhaps for the first time,
> that there is much more going on in the visible and in the invisible
> world than he has been aware of before. "Surely the LORD is in this
> place, and I was not aware of it."[2]

I showed Carol my "find," and we wept together, realizing that in the middle of this earthquake in our lives, we have been very unaware of God's presence, but that doesn't mean He isn't here. We were encouraged to know that Jacob felt the same way.

The image of the ladder between earth and heaven reminds us that there is activity going on in the unseen world. Have the demons been fighting to destroy our family? Have they been in strategy meetings in the invisible world, figuring out how to take us out — starting with our son, assuming the "trickle-down impact" will tempt us to quit serving Jesus?

One of my favorite visual images of the apostle Peter comes from John 6. People had been following Jesus out of curiosity and because they got free food and saw some eye-popping miracles. But then Jesus began explaining the real reason He was on earth — to reconcile us to His Father in heaven — and His bizarre message about people needing to eat His flesh and drink His blood in order to have eternal life was incomprehensible and offensive to most. Many of His followers said, "This is a tough teaching, too tough to swallow."[3] When Jesus added that no one was capable of following Him unless the Father willed it, many disciples deserted Him for good.

Jesus then turned to the twelve handpicked apostles and asked, "Do you also want to leave?"[4] Peter's response has been my key question while walking through this personal journey of unspeakable pain and deep grief. It fills me with sincere respect and with brotherly affection for the irrepressible Peter, the sanguine disciple who often acted without thinking. He answered Jesus' query with his own heartfelt question: "Master, to whom would we go? You have the words of real life, eternal life. We've already committed ourselves, confident that you are the Holy One of God."[5]

I agonized over the overwhelming journey ahead of us — Jason's current incarceration and our desperate fears for his safety, along with his upcoming trial. I grieved over the needs of his wife and stepdaughters — Chelsea was seven then; Hannah four. There were monumental legal fees and a great need to continue being active in ministry so the bills could be paid. That need for economic stability was combined with the desire to curl up in the fetal position and disappear, which was only intensified by the haunting question, *If people in my audiences knew I was the mother of a murderer, would they even want me to be their speaker?*

I drew comfort from Peter. I could almost see his furrowed brow and the questioning look on his face. I could feel the heaviness of his potential loss. I understood the sincerity of his simple response when he said, "Master, to whom would we go?" *Where else did I have to turn in this dark hour?*

I found myself sometimes angry, often hurt, always broken — but the bottom line of my heart was this: *Lord, where would I go if I turned away from You? If I didn't have You, I would have nothing. I have nowhere to turn, so while I'm pounding Your chest with my hurt, pain, and anger, please know that I am still facing You, still leaning into the warmth of Your embrace, not sure I can trust You, but knowing You are all I have. If I left You, I would be completely aimless and lost. So while I feel devastated by what You have allowed to happen, I still cannot resist pressing into the comfort of Your strong arms. I am angry that I am not resisting You more, because I know You could have stopped this thing from happening—but I have nowhere else to go.*

Gene continued our first week's chronicle:

> Carol and I both feel more empowered because we've gotten a small
> mental picture of the battle that is going on around us. We are in
> pain, but we are not giving up. We are engaging in this battle. We will
> choose life. We will choose hope.

But first we got mad. In fact, I had an all-out temper tantrum with Satan. The irony of the situation plagued me. *Could the Enemy have taken my son's strongest attribute—his sense of righteousness—and twisted it into making him believe he was destroying evil?* The more I contemplated, the angrier I got. *Did Satan, in his destructive, conniving way, also take a look at my ministry as a writer and a Christian public speaker and say, "Let's wipe out the parents along with the kid. If I can get to the kid, the parents will be immobilized too."*

I got so angry, I screamed out loud, "Satan, you can come after me, but don't put a finger on my child! I command you, in the name of Jesus Christ and His shed blood on the cross, to leave Jason Kent alone. Get away from him! You are despicable and disgusting! You are a loser! You are a DONE DEAL! You have only a little while longer to leave your mark and I know the end of your story! We win! You lose! Leave my family alone!"

My anger against the real enemy felt empowering. It helped me to pray with passion. I finally had a good reason for being on all fours pounding the floor!

When we fully understand that we are in a spiritual battle, that the world is not our home, just a "stopping off" place, we can begin to get excited about having a short time to engage in the battle raging around us. The Enemy wants us to waste our time generating anger toward others, ruminating over personal betrayals and over injustices due to sickness, accidents, and evil. He wants to destroy our ability to function productively and to disengage us from inspiring others to be Christ-followers. He wants us to give up and die or to control everything around us in such a tight-fisted manner that we're tied up in ridiculous knots.

The most freeing thing I did in the hours following the devastating blow at 12:35 A.M. was to activate my brain and decide that I would *not* let the Enemy win this round. I *would* choose hope. I *would* choose faith in unthinkable circumstances. If I practiced "eternity thinking," I could even glimpse beyond the end of my son's life. I could see further than the suffering of this situation with all of its losses.

I wrote to my family that night: "Included in this walk through the valley of what feels like death is an awareness of His presence I have never experienced before. I can almost hear the sound of angel wings."

THE POWER *of* UNTHINKABLE CIRCUMSTANCES

Looking back on the beginning of our crisis, I am now able to see how much power is released when we are in the middle of a totally unexpected situation that cannot be reversed. As days became weeks and weeks became months, Gene and I began to uncover the hidden treasure in our unthinkable circumstances.

- *We realized the world is in a mess.* In fact, we experienced as never before what it feels like to live in a chaotic, fallen world. Horrible things happen to people. Life-altering changes come into the lives of good,

Christian people who are trying their best to be Christ-followers and point others to the faith.

- *We asked for help.* Being in a situation that was totally out of our control forced us to seek wise counsel. It made us listen to advice and evaluate alternatives. Instead of following our gut feelings and making educated guesses, we sought assistance. This was a new response for me, because even though I had been a Christian for forty-five years, my natural tendency was not to depend on others, not even on my sisters and brothers in Christ. I was used to being the "strong" one, the self-sufficient one. I had a lot to learn about being "poor in spirit."

- *We recognized that everything trivial was just that—trivial.* Spilling a full cup of coffee on white carpeting was not a big deal. Running out of ink in the printer when an important letter had to be in the mail immediately was not a huge issue. The great debate over the new flooring in the church sanctuary was not a matter worthy of gigantic amounts of emotional energy. Compared to the "elephant" in our lives, everything else was less significant. It felt good to realize that "sweating the small stuff" was a ridiculous waste of time and energy. Having a measuring stick in our lives that helped us understand the difference between what was inconsequential and what was important proved to be freeing.

- *We admitted that our sense of control was an illusion.* I am a firstborn of six preacher's kids and grew up in a home where my father always said, "The oldest child in the house at any given time gets to be the boss." With my background as the chief babysitter for four younger sisters and a younger brother, I was very used to being in charge, and control came naturally to me. I was a people-pleaser and loved to do things perfectly and to be known as a competent person who "got the job done well." I was obsessive-compulsive about following through with my personal goals and would often work on projects for ridiculously long hours, having little respect for getting sleep or setting realistic expectations of my limits. Much of the time, I felt like there was nothing I couldn't "handle" or "manage." I was wrong.

- *We were humbled as never before.* Often my goals (and Gene's too) were spiritual in nature, which probably made us even more frustrated when we faced this huge tragedy with our son and hoped that God would be more direct with His answers to our questions. I realized that there was a part of me that thought, *Don't I deserve better than this after all I've done for the Lord? I love Him so much; why is He letting me be crushed like this?* I learned quickly that I wasn't unique and that pain is pain is pain. And I needed comfort, like a baby.

- *We had to affirm or reject our faith.* For years I had been telling audiences that God is good and He is trustworthy. "No matter what happens to you, God has your best interests in mind," I preached. "He will never walk away from you. He is your advocate. He is your provider. He is your victor."

During the early days of our crisis, I wondered about *all* of this. Where was God on the Sunday afternoon when my son shot Douglas Miller Jr.? Was God busy with affairs in the Middle East that day? Was He preoccupied with the issue of international terrorism? Was He distracted by a worldwide crisis? I agonized, "God, since You are omnipresent, why didn't You give Jason a flat tire that would have prevented him from entering that parking lot? Lord, why didn't You make his vehicle break down between Panama City and Orlando? You had six-and-a-half hours! Why didn't You *stop* this awful thing from happening?"

Gene and I were reeling from the shock and the loss of our son's future, and we were also grieving for the unspeakable loss the Miller family was experiencing. In a deeply personal way we realized that when unthinkable circumstances enter your life, there comes a point when you either stand by what you believe or you walk away from it. Over time, we chose the powerful reaffirmation of our foundational posture in the universe: God was God and we were not. We were utterly dependent on Him, and if we were to continue living with a sense of purpose and passion, we knew that our only hope was in His infinite mercy and His unshakable plan for redemption regardless of sin, sorrow, and shame.

God's Power in *Your* Circumstances

I sincerely hope that nothing has happened to you as horrible as learning that your child has committed murder. But with unthinkable circumstances, comparison is irrelevant. Is what happened in my family worse or better than learning that your daughter has a terminal illness or that your spouse is leaving you or that a disability will change the course of your plans and dreams? It doesn't matter. What matters is, *What will you do in response?* Will you curl up in that alluring fetal position or will you struggle on to find God, hope, purpose, and passion amid your circumstances?

1. "Unthinkable circumstances" look different for each individual. In your own experience, current or past, what are some of the challenging circumstances you've encountered, and what were the feelings you experienced as a result? What are some of the ways you have expressed and dealt with those feelings — either constructively or destructively?

2. What's going on in your prayers these days? Look back through this chapter and notice that begging prayers — the "wind-whipped waves" that James urges us to get past — are entirely normal when we're in shock and pain. Notice the ups and downs of my prayer life during this early stage. If your prayers are a "mess," take heart. Is there anything in what I said to God that you'd like to say to Him? Why not write a heartfelt prayer to God? Writing helps me like nothing else when my thoughts are in a jumble.

3. Are you asking for help from other people? If not, what keeps you from asking? (Embarrassment and self-reliance are possibilities.) Carefully consider what might benefit you most right now (and at each stage of your journey through unthinkable circumstances): Professional advice? A shoulder to cry on (literally)? Help running errands or keeping your household or business in order? A weekend away? Financial support? Whom can you ask to help you get what you need?

4. Do you tend, like me, to try to keep your world under your control? If so, what are some of your typical ways of trying to achieve that feeling of personal power? Why might it be good (rather than horrible) to accept that such control is an illusion?

5. Think about the idea of living in a chaotic, fallen world where bad things happen. Does that idea drive you toward God or away? I wrote, "In a deeply personal way we realized that when unthinkable circumstances enter your life, there comes a point when you either stand by what you believe or you walk away from it." Where are you right now on this choice about standing or walking away?

6. Discovering the power and the invaluable lessons found in unthinkable circumstances usually takes a great deal of time. If you can already articulate some of the things you've learned and ways you've grown, write them down as a testament to God's faithfulness even amid devastation and sorrow. If you have no idea what your circumstances are telling you, gently let yourself "off the hook" and *accept* that your experience is a *process*.

$\mathcal{L}$AYING ISAAC DOWN

The Power *of* Relinquishment

We can hug our hurts and make a shrine out of our sorrows
or we can offer them to God as a sacrifice of praise. The choice is ours.
—RICHARD EXLEY

THE FRONT PAGE OF THE *Orlando Sentinel* PICTURED A FAMILIAR face — my son's. But the headline was something I could not have imagined reading in my worst nightmares:

BLEMISH FOR NAVY OFFICER — MURDER CHARGE IN ORLANDO SHOOTING

The article reported:

> Jason Kent crewed on the U.S. Naval Academy's offshore sailing team. His love for water was supposed to take him this week to the Pacific Ocean and his first duty as an officer aboard a ship anchored in Honolulu. But the young lieutenant might never again go to sea. He spends his days in the Orange County Jail awaiting trial on a first-degree murder charge.
>
> An officer and a gentleman, Kent won't say a word about the burst of gunfire that killed his wife's ex-husband.[1]

We were also told that when J.P. fired multiple shots outside a busy restaurant on the afternoon of October 24, he sat at attention for hours following his arrest, unlike almost any other person investigators had observed in similar circumstances. The next day, J.P.'s attorney told him he could not talk to anyone about the details of the crime — including me, Gene, and April — because we would be called as witnesses to his mental state prior to the incident.

It took seventeen days for our local paper, the *Port Huron Times Herald*, to pick up the news of our son's arrest. A reporter repeatedly called our home requesting an interview, and we consistently refused comment. The tension in the house was thick. Every time there was a knock at the door and each time the phone rang, we wondered if it was a journalist.

People who knew us personally had begun hearing the story, and if they were acquainted with Jason, it was impossible for them to believe that this deplorable thing could have happened. They had a great need to call and verify the facts and express their grief to us as they simultaneously verbalized condolences and wept with us. After a while, we knew that when a call came from a relative or a friend who was receiving the news for the first time, it would take approximately one hour to go over the details and allow enough time for their questions, expressions of sympathy, and for their need to linger on the phone long enough so they knew we understood the depth of their concern. These calls were necessary, and often they were comforting, but they were emotionally exhausting.

Six days after Jason's arrest, April and the girls were able to have their first visit with him for the maximum allowable two hours, through a thick Plexiglas partition. Gene flew to Florida that Saturday night to help April and the girls begin their move from Panama City to a home closer to the jail in Orlando. I had plans to fly to Florida on Thursday to see my son and to meet with the attorney and with Dr. Gutman, the psychiatrist who was going to interview Jason.

It was late afternoon on the Tuesday before I left when the phone rang. The digitized message told me the call was coming from an institution and asked if I was willing to accept the charges. It was my son. J.P. was weeping and sounded very frightened.

"Mom, I've just been beaten up by ten guys here at the jail. They jumped me and started kicking me in the face when I walked back into the cell following my meeting with Dr. Gutman. My two front teeth are broken off and these guys stole all my stuff. They took my deodorant, soap, and toothpaste." He paused, and I heard a desperate sob.

I could hardly catch my breath. "Do you know if you have any broken bones?"

"I don't think so," he said, "but I'm pretty messed up. I have a lot of cuts and bruises. They just kept kicking me in the head."

"Why did they do this?" I stammered.

"One of the COs (corrections officers) was with them while I was out for my meeting with Dr. Gutman. The officer lied and told the men that my crime was racially motivated; he said I had killed an African-American man and his little girl, execution style. Evidently it's common for some of the COs and other prisoners to rile up the inmates by spreading false rumors that will cause agitation. The men responded to these lies by beating me when I was returned to the cell."

Choking on my tears, I sputtered, "Oh, son, I wish I could hold you in my arms right now. Dad is already in Orlando and you'll see him tomorrow. Because he's visiting from out of state, the authorities will allow him a special visit — but only for fifteen minutes."

We cried together that day. A mom and her boy, eleven hundred miles apart, embarking on a journey they never anticipated. Sixty seconds before the call ended, the digitized voice reminded us that our conversation was coming to a conclusion. "Jason, I love you. Dad and I are here for you. I wish I could fix this. I wish I could be with you right now."

The digitized voice came on again with a fifteen-second warning that the call was about to end. "I'm praying for you, son, and I will see you in a couple of days."

"I love you too, Mom." *Click.* The conversation was cut off abruptly by the institutional telephone system.

I was at my desk as the call ended and I heard a deep, guttural wailing sound coming out of my deepest being. "Oh, dear God, why didn't You protect him? Why did You let him get kicked in the head by angry, agitated inmates? How much more pain do You think I can bear? I feel so powerless, God! I don't know how to help my son. *Please* take care of him!"

I felt a mixture of ferocious anger and overwhelming fear. The situation was going from bad to worse.

After Gene visited April and Jason's home for the last time, he wrote in his journal:

> The darkness of our situation hangs like a shadow over everything. I flew to Panama City with my brother and we packed Jason and April's earthly goods into a big U-Haul and drove the six-and-a-half hours to Orlando. My most difficult moment while packing was seeing Jason's half-eaten twenty-fifth birthday cake, with the burnt candles still on top. I couldn't throw it out, so I stuffed it in a box with pots and pans. It was an odd feeling — like maybe if I kept the cake, my son would show up at the door and we'd finish eating it together.

Gene's brief visit with Jason the next day took place, instead, through the thick Plexiglas, with a guard just a few feet away. Gene told me later, "He looks bad. Bruises are covering his face. Both of his eyes are black. Gashes and nicks are in his chin and jaw, and his two front teeth are broken off. He's a broken young man. We both cried for several minutes before we could even talk."

"SPEAK *to* US, GOD!"

Along with our overwhelming grief and fear, we were keenly aware that there was another family in deep pain over the loss of a son. How could we have gotten into such a mess? What was God asking us to do? How we longed to hear directly from heaven!

Abraham heard more than once, including at the most dreadful moment of his life when he had a knife raised against his own son. The precious child God had given him and Sarah in their old age was to be an integral part of God's plan for His chosen people. Through Isaac, God had promised, Abraham would have more descendants than there were stars in the sky.

But first, Scripture tells us,

God tested Abraham. God said, "Abraham!"

"Yes?" answered Abraham. "I'm listening."

He said, "Take your dear son Isaac whom you love and go to the land of Moriah. Sacrifice him there as a burnt offering on one of the mountains that I'll point out to you."

Abraham got up early in the morning and saddled his donkey. He took two of his young servants and his son Isaac. He had split wood for the burnt offering. He set out for the place God had directed him. On the third day he looked up and saw the place in the distance. Abraham told his two young servants, "Stay here with the donkey. The boy and I are going over there to worship; then we'll come back to you."

Abraham took the wood for the burnt offering and gave it to Isaac his son to carry. He carried the flint and the knife. The two of them went off together.

Isaac said to Abraham his father, "Father?"

"Yes, my son."

"We have flint and wood, but where's the sheep for the burnt offering?"

Abraham said, "Son, God will see to it that there's a sheep for the burnt offering." And they kept on walking together.

They arrived at the place to which God had directed him. Abraham built an altar. He laid out the wood. Then he tied up Isaac and laid him on the wood. Abraham reached out and took the knife to kill his son.[2]

That whole mental picture sends shivers of horror up my spine. It seems so bizarre and so matter-of-fact. So brutal and so insane. Abraham tied up his only child, the son God promised, the one who was to make him so fruitful, and he took up his knife to *kill* him? *And God told him to do this?*

I'm sorry, but I don't think I could do that. It isn't natural. It isn't normal. It sounds like the craziest, most far-out, nonsensical, and horrific thing a parent could do to a child. *Why? What would the purpose be? What a waste of human life! What a terrible example to set for others! What is the deeper meaning? Is there a meaning?*

Author Larry Richards helped me make some sense of this. "Abraham was willing to offer his son Isaac because he was convinced that God could raise Isaac from the dead if that were necessary to keep His promises."[3] In other words, Abraham trusted in God's faithfulness so completely that he was willing to surrender what he deeply loved without being able to envision a specific or positive outcome. In an act of strong faith and total trust in God, Abraham made the decision to *lay his Isaac down*.

> Just then an angel of GOD called to him out of Heaven, "Abraham! Abraham!"
>
> "Yes, I'm listening."
>
> "Don't lay a hand on that boy! Don't touch him! Now I know how fearlessly you fear God; you didn't hesitate to place your son, your dear son, on the altar for me."
>
> Abraham looked up. He saw a ram caught by its horns in the thicket. Abraham took the ram and sacrificed it as a burnt offering instead of his son.
>
> Abraham named that place GOD-Yireh (GOD-Sees-to-It). That's where we get the saying, "On the mountain of GOD, he sees to it."
>
> The angel of GOD spoke from Heaven a second time to Abraham: "I swear — GOD's sure word! — because you have gone through with this, and have not refused to give me your son, your dear, dear son, I'll bless you — oh, how I'll bless you! And I'll make sure that your children flourish — like stars in the sky! like sand on the beaches! And your descendants will defeat their enemies."

Long before Isaac was born, God had given this same man detailed directions and a whole series of wonderful promises:

- Leave your country, your people and your father's household and go to the land *I will* show you.
- *I will* make you into a great nation and *I will* bless you.

- *I will* make your name great, and you *will* be a blessing.
- *I will* bless those who bless you, and whoever curses you I will curse; and all peoples on earth *will* be blessed through you.[4]

How I longed to hear God's audible voice like this in the middle of my own wilderness experience. It has often appeared to me that God gives very detailed direction to a few of His favorite people, and I want to be one of them! But God has never spoken to me out loud. I have friends who tell me God speaks to them, that they get a word from Him. But He has never communicated with me in that way. He usually speaks to me through Scripture. Sometimes He speaks to me through people who spend a lot of time in His presence. And occasionally, when I am meditating on God's Word and on His character, He speaks to me through an inner impression of the heart. Now, more than ever, I wanted direction about what to do for my son from a very confident, authoritative voice, and I was feeling tremendous frustration with not being able to figure out God's leading. "God, *please* speak to me like you did to those Bible characters," I found myself pleading. "I am *desperate* for direction."

LESSONS *from* ABRAHAM

As a significant biblical character, Abraham helps me identify the role of faith in reestablishing a trust-filled relationship with God. He also helps me to see God's plan to repair the damage that has been done by sin. There are some important markers in Abraham's life that can help all of us understand how to find hope in the middle of unthinkable circumstances.

- Abraham lived his life as a nomad, not sitting in an ancient seat of power.

It's a great reminder that even when it appears that we are going nowhere in the middle of our impossible circumstances, God has a plan, and God revealed that plan to Abraham when he needed to know what to do next. As Gene and I felt overwhelmed with how to best help our son, there were many days when it felt like we were in no-man's land trying to understand what God wanted us to do, but no promising master plan seemed to be emerging.

- Abraham failed the faith-test more than once, but his faith grew as
  he experienced more of God.

I can certainly identify with the way Abraham wanted to "help God out" with the master plan. Abraham failed as a husband when he begged Sarah to pretend that they weren't married and then allowed her to be taken into the king's household. It was a shocking request, and it meant that Sarah was installed in the harem of a pagan ruler. In spite of Abraham's betrayal, God protected Sarah's virtue.

Abraham also paid for his lack of faith big-time when he fathered a son by Hagar, Sarah's maid. This time, the idea was initiated by Sarah, but it wasn't God's idea. Later, Abraham's heart was deeply broken when he had to send his son Ishmael away after conflict arose between Sarah and Hagar.

When God says, "Trust me with the impossible," we have an automatic impulse to use our human brain to figure out how God would do the job if He were in our position. At the root of that response is a lack of faith, trust, and assurance that God can be counted on, as well as a certain arrogance that our self-reliance is of any value whatsoever. In our personal crisis, my assumption was that God wanted Gene and me to use our connections with people to resolve Jason's desperate straits. But, in this case, we were wrong.

- Abraham, when faced with the biggest test of his life, chose faith.

The story in Genesis 22 has baffled me as a parent and as a Christian. Why would God ask a father to lay his child on an altar and sacrifice him as a burnt offering? On the surface, it seems like a horrific, evil suggestion; but *God* is the one making the request. So I bring to this passage everything I know to be true about God, and I know God loves people and that He has their best interests in mind, even when the circumstances don't look like it.

Abraham had been walking with God a long time; he and God had some history. Abraham had heard God's voice before, so he knew this voice was indeed *God's* voice, not that of an imposter. Abraham also had past experience with failing faith-tests and doing things his own way, which resulted in some lessons learned the hard way. He was now at a trust level with God that did not necessitate room for "pause." He simply obeyed.

As I have looked more closely at the life of Abraham and the journey he made with his son from Beersheba to Mt. Moriah, two things have grabbed my attention. God had told him to take the son he loved and to go to Moriah to *worship*. He was to offer God's promise for his future, his son, as a sacrifice. And the Bible says *he got up early* to begin this trip. Abraham knew the purpose of the trip was to worship his God by sacrificing his son, and he was so enthusiastic about following God's instructions, he started the trip *early* in the morning. If I had been in that situation, I would have left at the latest possible time, hoping God would tell me He changed His mind and we could cancel the trip.

After traveling for three days, the man and his son arrived at their destination and built the altar. Abraham placed the wood he had split on the altar, and then he tied up his son and "laid his Isaac down." At that moment he relinquished his own desires, dreams, plans, and hopes for his Isaac's future and made the sacrifice an act of worship to the God he trusted with a confidence so strong that even if God allowed his son to die, Abraham knew God could raise him from the dead.

HEART SACRIFICES

I had always thought I had a robust and vibrant faith. Now, I wondered, *did I really?* Would my love for God and my desire to worship Him prevail in the midst of the most devastating circumstances I'd ever faced?

I know that Jason Kent is not a picture of Isaac in Genesis 22. Isaac was born in sin, because he was human, but there is nothing in this passage that leads us to believe he was laying his life down because of his own sin. He demonstrated total trust in his own father. My son, on the other hand, was guilty of taking the life of another man. My son was not like Abraham's son, but Jason Kent was my personal "Isaac." God seemed to be asking me to lay down my "claim" to him in complete trust and submission, even though everything in my mother's heart was screaming, "There must be something I can do to spare my son, to spare my own heart this crushing grief! This can't be happening!" But it *was* happening. And my own heart's desires were what I was being asked to sacrifice on the altar.

I also recognized that I had a large amount of personal pride, high expectations for my only child's future, natural desires to have a "normal" family with holiday reunions that included grandchildren opening presents around our Christmas tree, followed by a big turkey dinner and joyful conversation. My "Isaac" was filled with hopes and dreams of an idyllic future for our happy little Christian family. My "Isaac" was also a big pile of *expectations* that suddenly weren't going to materialize. Would I honor God by continuing to love and trust Him in these utterly unthinkable circumstances, or would I spend my days trying to direct an outcome that was so clearly beyond my control?

In *Radically Obedient, Radically Blessed,* Lysa TerKeurst writes:

> No one understands the concept of offering it all to God better than Abraham. . . . When God commanded Abraham to lay his only son on the altar . . . I am sure Abraham fully expected to plunge the dagger through Isaac. It would be an end . . . the death of a dream. Yet, Abraham was willing to give up the son he loved to the God who loved him more, and God blessed him . . . Abraham walked away having experienced God in a way few ever do. God wants to know if we're willing to give up what we love to Him who loves us more. He desires for us to open our fists and trust Him with absolutely everything.[5]

The key is to fully engage our hearts in understanding "the God who loves us more." I kept wondering, *the God who loves us more than what?* It took me a while to speak the answer out loud. He's the God who loves us *more than we love our Isaac.* Slowly, it dawned on me that one of my initial steps in making a heart sacrifice was to internalize the belief that God loves me even more than I love my son. That was a wild and radical thought because I love my son so much. I hurt for

Jason Kent so much. I ache for his losses of holding his wife and children in his arms. I agonize over the life he took and over his inability to change what happened. I grieve for the loss of his prestigious career with the U.S. Navy and of his ability to support his family financially.

But God loves me more than I love my son. He loves my son more than I do. Could that be possible? If so, then perhaps I could begin to ease my grip on these sad circumstances as my first move toward the altar.

I had much to learn about heart sacrifices. As defined by the dictionary, a *sacrifice* is "an act of offering to a deity something precious, something offered in sacrifice; it's surrender of something for the sake of something else, something given up."[6] True heart sacrifices involve:

- identifying something precious to us (our Isaac)
- letting go of our control over the situation, event, or the person as an act of worship
- embracing God's love in the process of the release
- resting in the outcome, even if in this lifetime we are not allowed to understand the reason behind the need for the sacrifice and the pain involved

A heart sacrifice is not a formula that can be mastered. It is a decision that is intrinsically tied to the personal relationship between us and our God. It is born out of a trust that is developed in spending time communicating with an Abba Father who loves us more than we love our Isaac.

The high value of our Isaac is what makes the sacrifice so demanding, because we don't know ahead of time if we'll get our Isaac back. Something it took me a while to understand is that God has never forced me to make a heart sacrifice. He has never demanded my allegiance or made me "give up" an Isaac just to play with my emotions. He has always allowed the choice to be mine. And that is precisely why the decision is so difficult. He lets me decide if I will make laying my Isaac on the altar an act of worship, where I lift up my heart in total trust in Him and release my grip on the object of my sacrifice.

ANOTHER KIND *of* ISAAC EXPERIENCE

I met Lorie when I was leading a Speak Up With Confidence Seminar in Louisville, Kentucky. She was effervescent, energized, and vibrant — a gifted communicator who was interested in doing more to hone her skills in public speaking. Later, she shared her story with me.

> When I was seventeen, I was captain of the dance/color guard team at school, and everything in my life was going well. At least I thought so. Every Friday night I would pour myself into a uniform that clung to every curve of my body. Between my studies, the practices, my need to look good in that uniform, and other aspects of my active life, I became overwhelmed. Something had to go. So I chose to quit eating.
>
> During football season of my senior year, my one meal of the day consisted of a baked potato, eaten with barbecue sauce. Initially, the hunger pangs were a nuisance, but they slowly turned into an inner reward, a private trophy of self-discipline. Often, I chose to skip that measly meal on Fridays so my stomach would feel lighter for the game that evening.
>
> As the season ended, the pace of life slowed down and I thought I could relax my food restrictions a little. But I quickly discovered the exact habit I had welcomed into my life to get control had escaped the box I had created for it, and it was now controlling me. My thoughts were constantly filled with food issues: *Will the party I'm going to have food? How can I escape having to eat in public?*
>
> Unable to always avoid eating in a public place, my anorexia soon developed into bulimia. If I sat down to a family meal in a restaurant, I would quickly assess the contents of the plate. Within seconds I knew exactly what to eat first, second, and last in order to reduce the amount of food that would be processed by my body before I could purge myself. This routine lasted for months — until someone noticed.
>
> Gayle, the director of a girl's mission organization at my church, entered my life, and it didn't take long for her to confront me about my

bulimia. I denied I had a problem. She encouraged me to meet with her weekly to go through a workbook on eating disorders. Gayle promised that as long as she and I met together, she would not tell my parents about my problem. With that promise, I kept our appointments.

But we came to a point in our meetings where Gayle knew I needed more help than she could offer and she told me it was time for me to tell my parents. I could have died. It was crushing to think of telling my parents that their daughter was not as "perfect" as they once thought. This confession was the hardest thing I have ever done in my life, but it led to professional counseling that ultimately saved my life.

The counseling began toward the end of my senior year of high school. I tried to be honest, but I also knew that unless my counselor gave me a clean bill of health, my parents would be hesitant to allow me to leave for college. I answered all of the questions not only to the best of my ability, but exactly as I knew I should in order to convince everyone that I was "healed." It worked. Six months later I had finished my treatment and I was ready to start college life.

Despite my lies, what the counselor told me did sink in. I changed a lot of my habits, but no matter how much I told myself I was healed, deep down inside I was afraid I could never fully release my disorder. Fear and hopelessness were my constant companions.

One night I visited a friend who had just made brownies. They looked good and I noticed how relaxed she was while eating them. She honestly looked like she was *enjoying* the brownie; it was not her enemy as it had so long been mine. I couldn't resist. I ate one. The rest of the night passed as usual until I went to bed.

I couldn't sleep. All I could think about was that brownie lying there in my stomach. I became overwhelmed with the desire to go purge myself and get rid of it, yet inside I was screaming, "No, God, I don't want to do this again." I lay there and battled with my own mind. For the first time I realized that I *could not stop*. I had absolutely no control. This disorder was going to take my life.

At that point I resigned myself to dying because I knew I could never be normal again. However, I couldn't die in such a stupid way—over an eating disorder. So I decided the best thing to do was to "accidentally" die and end it all.

For weeks, I sped up while driving home from classes. I knew exactly what spots in the road were known for their high rate of wrecks. No one would know my "accident" was on purpose. Yet each time my foot pressed the accelerator and my hands gripped the wheel tighter, something stopped me. Something in me would not allow me to go through with it.

That is when I broke. I hated myself. I was hopeless. I was pitiful. I could do nothing right. I could not eat like a normal person. I was too weak to fight the disorder, and now I was too stupid and scared to even kill myself.

One evening after another failed attempt, I went home to take a shower. I pulled the radio into the bathroom with me, and Ray Boltz was singing "The Anchor Holds." As I listened, the Lord broke my spirit. I collapsed on the floor of the shower, crumpled and crying, and I called out to God, "Oh Father, I have destroyed my life. I cannot go on living as I am. I have tried to fix everything and it only gets worse. Please, please save me."

That day I finally released my tight fists and "laid my Isaac down." Letting go of my control of my eating habits gave me a new sense of strength. While reading my Bible one day, I discovered Psalm 116:1-6: "I love GOD because he listened to me, listened as I begged for mercy. He listened so intently as I laid out my case before him. Death stared me in the face; hell was hard on my heels. Up against it, I didn't know which way to turn; then I called out to GOD for help: *Please, God!* I cried out. *Save my life!* . . . GOD takes the side of the helpless; when I was at the end of my rope, he saved me."[7]

Because He heard me, I am here today. I love Him more than I love my control. I finally chose to open my fists and let go, and on the altar of heart sacrifice, I said *Yes* to life and *No* to death.

LETTING GO *of* CONTROL

When I heard Lorie's story, it made perfect sense to me. I, too, was living in a place where I needed to *daily* choose life or death. My problem wasn't an eating disorder, but some days our situation threatened to extinguish my desire to live. It was exhausting to try to keep controlling household business, legal matters, my son's safety, news releases, and what people thought about what had happened.

Soon after the news of Jason's arrest hit our local papers, an acquaintance wrote to tell me that she had taken it upon herself to contact every ministry where I had ever spoken, every television and radio station where she knew I had been interviewed, and every Christian leader she thought I might know, to let them know what had happened to our family so they could pray for us. She then listed all of the contacts she had made "on our behalf." She never checked to verify the facts of the story with us. She simply told all of these key people what she had read in the papers because she knew they would want to know. After reading through her list, I realized this must have been a multiple-day job.

Frustrated and confused, I screamed out loud to my husband, "Don't people have anything else to do? They are getting a feeling of power out of announcing our bad news in the name of prayer requests, when they don't even have all of the facts straight. This is so wrong!"

My husband, Gene, is a unique personality. He never gets as animated as I do in the middle of an emotional outburst, nor does he "hit bottom" as far down as I do when things are not going well. He's steady, even, and controlled most of the time. Following my outburst that day, Gene took my hands in his two hands and said, "Carol, what's happened here is way out of our control. We are proactive people and we like to 'fix' things, but we can't change what's taken place or how this woman has responded to it. There's not one thing we can do to stop the rumors, the stories, the opinions, and the gossiping of people. We have to let it go. This is way beyond us."

I arrived in Florida on November 4, 1999, just in time to meet my husband for an appointment at the attorney's office for a face-to-face meeting with the man who, humanly speaking, would hold my son's future in his hands. It was a somber meeting. The rest of our son's life was at stake. This was not a case that would decide whether or not Jason pulled the trigger. He *did* pull the trigger in a public parking lot with multiple witnesses. Eyewitness testimony alleged that Jason Kent had *chased* Douglas Miller Jr. and shot him repeatedly — *in the back!*

The question was *why? WHY?* Why would a young man with a U.S. Naval Academy education, who had a flawless record, a compassionate heart for others, and orders from the U.S. Navy to go to a military base in Honolulu, Hawaii, as his first military assignment do something this bizarre? His orders to serve his country on a tropical island would be considered an enviable assignment. Why would he risk losing this opportunity? Why would he jeopardize the rest of his life? Why would he put his family's future in such peril? Why would a man highly trained in covert military activity shoot another man in broad daylight with witnesses all around him? Why would he make copious, obsessive notes about his plans, including what appeared to be a scheme to successfully flee the scene of the crime, and then do nothing to follow through? He was arrested without incident, having utilized none of the "props" he had brought along that the prosecutor would later claim he intended to use to get away with the shooting and dispose of the evidence. Nothing made any sense!

Gene and I immediately liked attorney Bill Barnett and his partner, Bert Barclay. We sensed Bill's sincere concern about Jason's future, and we believed he would do the best job he could to represent our son and get to the bottom of the *why* question. Many theories emerged. Jason was in the most intensive dive school the Navy offered at the time of the incident. We had heard there were hidden government studies on bizarre behavior that could follow dives the military men had after using mixed gases at extreme ocean depths. Perhaps the dive school in Panama City could offer us some background information that would prove useful.

Jason had also taken bodybuilding nutrients. Reports were surfacing on peculiar and sometimes dangerous behavior that would follow ingestion of

Ephedra, a commonly used, legal substance that was often added to powdered muscle enhancers and weight-control products sold in health food stores. We wondered if he could have been negatively affected by these products.

Did he begin to lose the ability to think rationally in part due to the huge time demands in his life? He was juggling the Navy dive school, a new marriage and two children, plus thirteen-hour round-trip drives from Panama City to Orlando every other weekend for the mandatory visits Chelsea and Hannah had with their father. Those drives were usually turnaround trips, and he would get back just in time to get up in the early hours of Monday morning for dive school. Since Jason started his plebe year at the academy five years earlier, he had never had a break from constant stress. *Did he mentally disintegrate under the extreme pressure?*

There was one significant additional question in our minds. *Had Jason become so obsessed and fearful for the safety of Chelsea and Hannah that he counted the cost and willingly sacrificed his own life for theirs?* Since his arrest, we have not yet been free legally to have a conversation with Jason about what he was thinking immediately before, during, and after the crime. In our depositions and testimony, however, Gene and I did talk about witnessing a profound change in our son's mental state prior to the murder. Several months after J.P. and April were married, they discovered that Douglas Miller Jr. was going through the legal process to seek unsupervised visits with his daughters. Up until this time all of the visits he had with Chelsea and Hannah were supervised by another adult, as mandated by the court in the custody arrangement between April and Douglas. Soon after Douglas initiated his motion for unsupervised visits, J.P.'s conversations with us changed markedly. He had always been a young man who talked animatedly about politics, issues, world events, and current family situations. With every call, we noticed that once the conversation turned to the children, Chelsea and Hannah, there was a tense anxiety within him. All he could talk about was his concern for them and his fear, should they have unsupervised visitation with their father.

We knew Jason believed that Douglas had a darker side than what he presented to many. Jason also believed April's detailed accounts of her own physical and psychological abuse by her first husband, as well as the horrors of alleged sexual abuse perpetrated against the children. Because Jason was, by nature, such a compassionate and protective man, we wondered if these mental and emotional burdens about what he believed might happen to his stepdaughters if he didn't intervene had caused him to become unglued.

Memories and unanswered questions haunted me. I remember the day J.P. came home from his special operations training at the Naval Academy with a cloud of uncertainty and anxiety hanging over his head. He said, "Mom and Dad, I am being trained to protect our citizens by taking the lives of men who are at war with the United States. I have had to ask myself if I'm capable of that. I am being trained with firearms as an expert marksman, and I've continued to wrestle with the fact that I am being taught how to kill. I'm a Christian and I don't know if I can take the life of another man." I watched my son deal with the issue of war and protecting helpless people from evil demagogues. He finally came to a resolution that if people were in danger, he could do what he was trained to do.

Gene and I are patriotic Americans who are deeply grateful for our military forces, but we wondered if the intensity of J.P.'s training, the sleep deprivation, and his obsession with believing the father of his stepdaughters was capable of sexual abuse contributed to his psychological demise on the fateful day he shot Douglas Miller Jr. Had his military training been partly responsible for twisting his mind into believing he was doing the only "right" thing?

J.P. seemed to become even more obsessed and anxious after the attorney he and April hired to fight Douglas's motion told them that they might not be successful. During this time, April said J.P. would sometimes curl up in an fetal-like ball on their bed and pound his fists saying he didn't know how to protect the girls. April, Gene, and I noticed that he was becoming increasingly obsessed by fear for the girls' safety, and it disturbed us that he seemed increasingly incapable of functioning with his characteristic affability and humor. We heard intense anxiety in his voice whenever we spoke with him.

Now with Jason behind bars only thirteen months after marrying April, we had far more questions than answers. Based on everything we knew about Jason's character and his spiritual life, however, we believed he had become so obsessively focused on saving Chelsea and Hannah from what he believed to be potential harm that he mentally unraveled. One of the psychiatrists who interviewed him after the crime firmly believed that J.P. had developed a severe obsessive-compulsive disorder that had irrevocably impaired his ability to think rationally. Gene and I believed there was only one reason for our son's actions and only one avenue for legal defense. He was severely temporarily mentally impaired at the time of the crime. We also knew that juries do not like the defense plea of "not guilty by reason of temporary insanity," and statistics told us it is a successful defense in only 5 percent of cases tried.

SEEING MY SON . . . FINALLY

The next morning I arrived at the huge compound called the Thirty-third Street facility and waited in line to request a special visit with my son. I'm not proud to tell you that I had never visited anybody in a jail before my son was arrested. I didn't know anyone who was incarcerated. To my knowledge, no one in our large extended family had ever been arrested for an illegal act, so I was totally unschooled in what I was about to experience.

The woman at the front desk was unhappy and agitated. When I made my request for a special visit, she indicated that the men in maximum security were only allowed one special visit for fifteen minutes, and I would only get my visit if they had an officer available who could bring Jason down. I told her I was willing to wait as long as necessary, but I needed to see my son before returning home to Michigan.

That morning began my journey of waiting in long visitation lines, being put on hold indefinitely when making calls to people in authority at the jail, and in general, realizing that if I didn't get a helpful person on my first call, I should wait for the shift change at the jail and hope to get someone who had more compassion on my second or third try.

About an hour after making my request to see Jason that morning I was ushered into a room with small cubicles that were outfitted with Plexiglas partitions. My heart was pounding so loudly I thought I could hear the beat.

Suddenly my son appeared. He was dressed in "blues," but not the naval uniforms I usually saw him in with all of the brass buttons and the decorative medals. There was a chain around his waist that was attached to both handcuffs. His ankles were in leg irons, with a chain between them, making his walk more like a shuffle than a stride.

As our eyes met briefly, they were brimming with tears. He looked down and the weight of the suffering and hurt, along with our knowledge of the ugliness of what had happened, came crashing in on both of us. It had only been three days since his beating, and portions of his face were still swollen and black and blue from the wounds. A cut on one of his ears was still oozing blood.

We both grabbed the old-fashioned black telephone receivers on either side of the thick glass. "Son," I stammered, "I love you. I want you to know there is nothing you could ever do that would take away my unconditional love for you." An armed guard stood about a yard away, listening in on our conversation.

J.P. looked up at me and through his sobs, he said, "Thank you, Mom. I love you so much." As he opened his mouth I could see what was left of his front teeth: jagged edges and pointy ends. As my boy looked up, I saw a blood clot in one of his eyes.

He was broken, hurt, sad, and beaten. And so was I. As I looked at my son behind the glass, I knew that there was nothing I could do about the circumstances that brought Jason to that place. There was no way to bring Douglas Miller back to life. There was no way to fix things and make life as it was before. That day I took the first step in "laying my Isaac down." I admitted to God that I was helpless to do anything to make this situation better. I sat in the parking lot of the Thirty-third Street facility and cried until I ran out of tears. I physically opened my hands, palm side up, and said:

> God, please help us not to waste this suffering. I could not go on living if I didn't believe I could trust You even in this. I give up my right to control the outcome of Jason's trial. I release his future to Your keeping, but God, even while I'm saying I want to relinquish my control, I want to take it back. So God, I will let go of my control for the

next minute, and if I make it that far, let's try for five more minutes, and maybe there will be a time when I will come to the end of one full day.

One of the next things I had to lay down, besides past events I was power-less to change, was my expectation for a speedy resolution to Jason's legal situa-tion. Waiting was to be the first requirement in my heart sacrifice — and I hate to wait! We were initially told that the earliest the trial would take place would be five months after Jason's arrest, but that it would more likely be at least a year later due to the amount of evidence that needed to be gathered, the psychologi-cal exams that would have to be evaluated, and the depositions that would need to be taken. I thank God now that I didn't know in advance how long the wait would be. My son's jury trial was postponed seven times over a two-and-a-half-year period. I had to wait thirty-three months after his arrest to even touch my only child again.

THE POWER *of* RELINQUISHMENT

Relinquishment is a poignant word. It means "to let go of, to cease to hold in the hand."[8] It means giving up my rights to control the person, dream, expectation, or preferred outcome of the object of my concern.

I'm not going to list the ten or twelve ways you can experience the power of relinquishment, because laying your Isaac down is not a pat little ten-step program. There is no medal or prize to win if you follow a specific set of instruc-tions. Relinquishing your "right" to hold your precious Isaac in your own hands is the most painful thing you will ever do. It seems as irrational as Abraham's decision to place his son on the altar. It goes against the grain of human self-reliance, and it seems wasteful of our perceived ability to fix things. But when we release our grasp, our relinquishment puts a stop to our manipulation of other people and releases the Holy Spirit to do the supernatural through the power of prayer. It's an act of trusting God when we cannot envision a positive outcome. But in the end, it's the only thing that works. I know. I have walked this road.

Over the past few years I have realized that there are two different categories of "Isaac experiences." Some "Isaacs" are losses that are thrust upon us, such as:

- being diagnosed with a terminal illness
- struggling with infertility
- death of a loved one
- loss of a job or a ministry position
- giving birth to a child with a disability
- an accident that results in a major life-change
- a financial reversal
- a child who has turned his or her back on what we have taught him or her
- an unwanted move to another home or to a different city
- a desire to marry, with no life partner in sight

A second category of "Isaac experiences" involves personal choices, such as:

- letting go of personal expectations of myself or someone else
- giving up a cherished dream for a greater good
- recovering from an addiction
- relinquishing our control over a child who is becoming an adult
- giving up my "right" to be in charge of my own life
- surrendering my ideal life for the reality of what I actually have
- forgiving a person who betrayed my trust
- embracing God's love when He doesn't rescue my hurting child
- longing for a more ideal spouse, but staying in a difficult marriage
- believing that God's promises are true when I am in a personal hell

You probably haven't received a middle-of-the-night phone call informing you that your child has been arrested for murder, but I'm sure of one thing: You *have* had to let go of a cherished person, opportunity, position, habit, or dream. It might be a situation that was thrust upon you due to an accident, relocation, illness, or change in ministry or work position. Or it might be something you cherished that you gave up with open hands because of a greater good or simply because you knew it was the right thing for you to do. Whatever the specifics were, it was a heart sacrifice — something you laid down and released at great personal cost.

At some time or another on our spiritual journey, each of us faces the challenge of laying an Isaac down. Like it or not (and who does?), the Christian life inherently involves "losing our lives" as Jesus did. A few days before His death, He compared His destiny to that of a grain of wheat: "Listen carefully: Unless a grain of wheat is buried in the ground, dead to the world, it is never any more than a grain of wheat. But if it is buried, it sprouts and reproduces itself many times over."[9]

A seed has to give up its familiar form as a seed, allow itself to be buried in the dark earth, and trust that God will bring new life — even lush life — when the seed sprouts. In the same way, we need to be willing to give up whatever is most familiar, comfortable, and precious to us, allow ourselves to sink into the darkness, and trust God to bring life out of what feels like death. This is the mystery of fruitfulness: Life multiplied many times over from what seems like death.

I thought my life was plenty fruitful before I laid my Isaac down: I had a thriving ministry, good friends, and a great family. I had a glowing picture in my mind of what a fruitful life J.P. could have as a husband, father, and naval officer. But God said, "Let the seed fall into the dark earth and die. Let Me choose the time and nature of the fruit." It has been the hardest thing I have ever done.

God's Power in *Your* Circumstances

No one I know has been exempt from "faith-tests." Whether these tests feel brutally incomprehensible, like Abraham's, or are simply "par for the course" of life as a follower of God, they seem to have at least one thing in common: letting go of control. We get to choose how we will go about this excruciating process. Will we honor God by continuing to love and trust Him regardless of our circumstances, or will we insist on trying to direct the outcome?

  1. Now or in the past, what has been your personal "Isaac" — the cherished person, thing, desire, habit, dream, or position you've

needed to relinquish in order for God to release His power? In what "category" have your most difficult Isaac experiences fallen — losses unexpectedly thrust upon you or personal choices that have required great sacrifice?

2. What have been some of your internal and external responses to the challenge to "trust God with the impossible"? When you think about relinquishing your Isaac, what do you find yourself doing? (Examples: Busying yourself so you don't have to think about it. Bargaining with God — "If I _____, then will You _____?" Eating. Succumbing to depression. Getting mad.) What would relinquishing your Isaac for five minutes involve? What about relinquishing your Isaac for a week?

3. When was the last time you felt *desperate* for divine direction? Did you receive it? If so, what surprised or comforted you? What has your experience of "hearing God's voice" been like through the years?

4. Review what "true heart sacrifices" involve on page 43. If you're currently facing an Isaac experience, what part of this difficult process are you in? What next step might you need to take in order to move closer to the altar where you can lay your Isaac down as an act of worship?

5. How do you respond to the idea that your life will be fruitful in proportion to your willingness to "lose your life," as Jesus taught? I wrote, "We need to be willing to give up whatever is most familiar, comfortable, and precious to us, allow ourselves to sink into the darkness, and trust God to bring life out of what feels like death. This is the mystery of fruitfulness: Life multiplied many times over from what seems like death." What are some of your experiences along these lines?

6. What would you like to say to God about everything this chapter has caused you to consider? Being completely honest — as I was when I prayed my first prayer of relinquishment in the jail parking lot — write out a prayer that expresses where you are now.

$\mathcal{W}$HY DIDN'T GOD DO SOMETHING?

The Power *of* Heartache

Heartache forces us to embrace God out of desperate, urgent need.
God is never closer than when your heart is aching.
—JONI EARECKSON TADA

WE WERE ENTERING A NEW PHASE OF OUR JOURNEY, AND WE had no idea how our small story would fit into God's Grand Story. Apart from a conviction that "there's-more-to-what's-happening-than-we-can-see-or-und erstand," we would have caved in and quit life. Still, there was one thing we had in abundance, and that was tears.

I wasn't prepared for the severe grieving of the people closest to us. Of the sixteen children my five siblings and I have among us, J.P. is the oldest cousin. He was the hero of his younger cousins and greatly enjoyed intellectual and spiritual bantering with the cousins closest to his age. As they became teenagers, he wrote letters encouraging them to keep their standards high, to live for things that mattered, and to stay morally pure. My sister, Joy, the mother of seven of J.P.'s cousins, told me a dark cloud settled over their home after the news of Jason's arrest. The whole family was in deep grief.

As Gene and I called our family members one by one, the sadness was great, and I would often slip away from the phone and let Gene finish the story. I couldn't bear to hear the pain in the voices on the other end of the line. After my nephew, Josh, got the news, my sister, Jennie, found him soberly playing and replaying portions of videotapes that recorded Jason's humorous antics and his meaningful verbal communications at previous family reunions. Each person coped in his or her own way. I found myself stopping at every framed picture of my son and outlining his face with my finger, while offering a desperate prayer-plea for his safety. We had different grieving rituals, but we were all mourning.

Even though life as we knew it had shattered, Gene and I still had the huge challenge of paying our own monthly bills and making sure Jason's legal expenses would be covered. We had made an arrangement with the attorney to pay a large initial fee for part of his retainer, followed by monthly amounts that were larger than mortgage payments. Gene had enjoyed a long and successful career working with investments and life insurance, but more than a year before J.P.'s arrest he had moved his office in with my office. He was downsizing his business considerably in order to take on the increasing responsibilities of running Speak Up Speaker Services, the speakers' bureau run through our office that helps to place approximately 150 Christian speakers with groups that need their services. He was also managing all of my public speaking engagements and taking care of all product sales at those events, so he was traveling with me at least three days a week. Because our financial stability was depending more and more exclusively on the ministry activities associated with Speak Up, Inc., I *had* to keep working.

In just two weeks I was to be one of the keynote speakers at the annual convention for MOPS, International, where an auditorium in Kansas City would be filled with more than two thousand mothers of preschoolers looking for tips on how to raise kids right and maintain their sanity in the process. The irony of speaking to this group of mothers only two weeks after my son had been arrested for murder was mind-boggling. The MOPS staff had no idea what I was going through. The program was so upbeat and focused on fun that it would have been inappropriate to share the depth of my pain with that crowd. I also was under strict instructions from Jason's attorney to not speak publicly about the case.

After arriving at the convention, I stayed in my room weeping late into the night and got up early the next morning to go over my notes and to pray for the courage to stand before those mothers. That day God provided a comforting companion for me in the form of one of my dearest friends, Cathy Gallagher. I had known Cathy since J.P. was a baby, and she had been one of the people Gene called early on to share our heartbreaking news. Cathy knew that this speaking event would be particularly challenging, and she drove four hours from her home in St. Louis to silently pray me through each speaking session, make eye contact when I shared a parenting illustration about J.P., and catch my tears when the sessions ended. She also taught me something important: When people are hurting, giving them the gift of our presence, without requiring lengthy conversation, is one of the kindest and most comforting gifts we can offer.

THE TRUTH *about* TEARS

I once heard a health-care professional speak about tears. She claimed that tears caused by laughter are very different than tears caused by sorrow. I didn't take notes on the composition of the differences between the two, but I know God created human beings who cry. I found comfort in the realization that the tears caused by sorrow matter so much to God that they even have a different consistency than "happy tears." It's how He designed us.

I knew a lot about the joyful kind of tears. I had often "laughed until I cried." I had enjoyed a remarkably happy life up to this point. However, our "Isaac experience" brought a whole new understanding of what it feels like to weep copiously with sorrowful, heartrending, unstoppable, and uncontrollable tears. I cried when I woke up in the morning. I cried when I heard Jason's favorite Michael W. Smith song on the radio. I cried when I saw his dive equipment in the basement. I cried when one of his best friends stopped by the house to ask how he was doing. I cried when I walked past his framed diploma from the U.S. Naval Academy, complete with a picture of the midshipmen tossing their hats into the air on that incredibly sunny and gloriously joy-filled graduation day in Annapolis, Maryland. I not only cried. I sobbed.

As a child, I learned that the shortest verse in the Bible is "Jesus wept."[1] Little did I know how comforting that verse would be to me later in life. In the middle of my crying binges, when I felt like I would literally drown in my feelings of deep personal loss, the memory of that short Scripture verse reminded me that it was okay to cry. If Jesus cried, it must be a good thing to weep.

I didn't always know that. I practiced "acting like a grown-up" from an early age, as I had a lot of responsibility for babysitting my five younger siblings and often had the role of wiping the tears of the crybabies who had stubbed a toe or had a spat with another sibling. As I grew older, I took pride in being able to handle small stresses and obstinate people. While I had a tender heart toward others, I didn't wear my heart on my sleeve, and I didn't like to let anybody know when I was hurting. I could handle things. I could deal with my own emotions. In fact, I rather prided myself on not being a burden to others.

This instinctive mode of being a "big girl" in the midst of challenging circumstances was my natural response even when my world felt like it had just fallen apart. I had certainly experienced some personal sadness in the past — the miscarriage of a second child that Gene and I desperately wanted, the loss of one of our dearest friends to cancer, two unwanted moves due to my husband's job transfers that removed me from purposeful and meaningful work and ministry. But in spite of these earlier losses, I was usually the person who helped others get through their tough times.

Now, my intense and unfamiliar feelings of unrelenting sorrow and depression caused me to feel shame for not having better "control" of my emotions. During the first few months after Jason's arrest became public knowledge, my worst moments were when I walked into our church on Sunday mornings. Heads would look up and conversations would cease. People didn't always know what to do or what to say. I could sense their discomfort about discussing "mundane" things in front of us. One by one friends would come up and hug me and, with tears in their eyes, say, "How are you doing? How are J.P. and April holding up?" Their tears unplugged my tears again and again. The usually "controlled Carol" was coming unglued. She wept a lot.

As I looked more closely at that little verse, "Jesus wept," I discovered that Jesus cried after being told that Lazarus had died. At first I wondered if Jesus was simply mourning the loss of His friend, but in reality, He seemed to be weeping for another reason. Martha ran to meet Jesus and said,

"Master, if you'd been here, my brother wouldn't have died."[2]

A little later Mary fell at His feet and said, "Master, if only you had been here, my brother would not have died."[3] Jesus saw Mary's tears and He also saw the other mourners. Then He asked where they put Lazarus. People in the crowd commented on Jesus' emotional response. Some thought His tears were because He loved Lazarus so much, but others had a different comment that some might call judgmental.

"Well, if He loved him so much, why didn't He *do* something to keep him from dying? After all, He opened the eyes of a blind man."[4]

I wondered why God didn't *do* something to keep my son from taking the life of another man. After all, He performed all of those miracles, including bringing Lazarus back to life. Did He choose *not* to intervene in the deadly altercation between Jason Kent and Douglas Miller Jr.?

My friend's baby granddaughter was recently diagnosed with a severe hearing loss and with cerebral palsy. Why didn't God *do* something to stop this from happening? The child's parents are some of the most dynamic, committed Christian leaders I know. They have made sacrificial service to God their highest priority, but their child has brain damage and severe, lifelong disabilities.

Why didn't God heal my friend, Nan, from the breast cancer that raged through her body over a five-year period? Nan prayed in faith believing that God would heal her from this disease. She encouraged the people around her, showed compassion to the needy, and mentored a prisoner who needed someone to care during the time he was incarcerated and after he was released. Nan was an exceptional Christian with a gift for evangelism. And she suffered and died. Why didn't God *do* something?

While I was ruminating over this age-old perplexing question, I went back to the Bible to read more of the context around the simple Scripture that tells us Jesus wept. After Mary approached Jesus following the death of Lazarus, the Scripture tells us, "When Jesus saw her sobbing and the Jews with her sobbing, *a deep anger welled up within him.* He said, 'Where did you put him?'"[5] Following the critical comment from people who thought Jesus should have done something to keep Lazarus from dying, the Bible says, "Then Jesus, *the anger again welling up within him,* arrived at the tomb."[6]

Jesus said, "Remove the stone."[7]

Martha is upset, but she follows her usual pattern by trying to manage and control, even in the process of grieving, and says, "Master, by this time there's a stench. He's been dead four days!"[8]

Jesus looks her in the eye and says, "Didn't I tell you that if you believed, you would see the glory of God?"[9] He again directs the people to take away the stone.

Jesus raises His eyes to heaven and prays, "Father, I'm grateful that you have listened to me. I know you always do listen, but on account of this crowd standing here I've spoken so that they might believe that you sent me."[10]

At that point Jesus shouted, "Lazarus, come out!"[11] When Lazarus emerged, he was wrapped from head to toe and he had a kerchief over his face. Jesus' response is simple and direct, "Unwrap him and let him loose."[12]

As I continued to ponder the reason for Jesus' tears, I looked for clues that would point to the rationale behind the simple sentence "Jesus wept."[13] At first it seemed elusive, and I realized that I had heard that verse for my entire life, but not until our crisis did I ever investigate *why* Jesus cried. Perhaps He wept for one or more of these reasons:

- His dear friend, Lazarus, had died. They had often talked together. They ate meals together. The home of Lazarus and his sisters was the closest thing to an earthly home Jesus ever had. He loved spending time with Lazarus. His friend had died and He was mourning.
- He also could have been mourning for the pain of Mary and Martha. Their tears were obvious and their questions were similar, "Master, if only you had been here, my brother would not have died." He loved these women and when our friends hurt, we hurt.
- Jesus might have been grieving over the lack of faith of the Jews who loved Lazarus and over the inability of Mary and Martha to see beyond the physical death of their brother to all that Jesus could provide for their family supernaturally. He perhaps expected that by this time they would "get" that He was capable of performing miracles.
- More than anything else, perhaps, Jesus was upset with the human

condition. When sin entered the world, physical death became
a reality. No longer did man have a limitless life on this earth.
Sickness, accidents, evil, death, and unspeakable circumstances were
present in the world. These facts of life had to be faced by every
human being. Were Jesus' tears and His anger because of the sad
state of the human condition?

I was comforted knowing that if Jesus wept for Mary and Martha's great
loss, He certainly was weeping with Gene and me too.

A FATHER'S TEARS

There was another man I often saw weeping. It was my husband. He would come
in after a three-mile run and I could see tears in his eyes. Gene and Jason were very
close as a father and son, and they often went jogging together during J.P.'s teen and
young adult years. They even challenged each other to run a half-marathon during
Jason's senior year at the Naval Academy, and they finished the race together.

One day I asked Gene to write about the tears I saw so frequently, and here
is what he journaled:

Growing up, I never saw my father cry. I saw him laugh at jokes, work
without complaint on the railroad, argue with my mother over "adult"
stuff; but I never, *ever*, saw him cry.

In 1974 my wife gave birth to our first and only child — a son. I
cried when he was born. I cried when he walked. I even shed some
tears when I heard him say, "Da Da." There were happy tears when
he started school. Joyful tears when he graduated from high school
with honors. Proud tears when he was granted an appointment to the
U.S. Naval Academy in Annapolis, Maryland.

Four years later, on graduation day, I again wept as my son
received his diploma and a congratulatory handshake from then
Vice President Al Gore. I also had wistful and happy tears on the
night of his marriage to April Dawn Miller. One chapter of his life

was ending, and a new chapter was beginning.

But in the early morning hours of October 25, 1999, I experienced a different kind of tears. Upon hearing that my son had just been arrested for committing first-degree murder, tears of anguish flooded over me. They wouldn't stop for any length of time, and they didn't begin to subside until several weeks later.

My tears were over all that was lost. My son's future. *His* lost dreams, hopes, and desires. *My* lost dreams for my only child and for all of the lost hopes and dreams of my daughter-in-law April. I also grieved for our new granddaughters, Chelsea and Hannah. And for Jason's grandparents, aunts and uncles, and cousins. I felt pain for the friends and peers who cared for our son and for his family. I grieved for the loss of my favorite running partner and for all of the future runs we might never have together.

Dads want to fix things for their kids — and I couldn't fix what happened in a parking lot at a Sweet Tomatoes Restaurant in Orlando, Florida, on a Sunday afternoon that could never be relived.

I found myself bristling when a well-meaning friend called with condolences and burst into an enthusiastic rendition of, "For we know that all things work together for good to those who love God, to those who are the called according to His purpose." Pl-e-e-e-e-ze! But my tears were more plentiful than my feelings of anger.

Where was God in this thing when it happened? Where was He in my life and in my son's life? My tears came from thinking about the unfixable and the seeming absence of my God. I still believed in God, but I was mystified by His choice not to intervene when He is omnipresent and He is all-powerful.

BROKENNESS *and* RESTORATION

Three weeks after Jason's arrest, Gene and I were facing one of many difficult decisions. One was in regard to an engagement I'd had scheduled for more than a year. Approximately 500 military wives and active duty women in the military from fifty-five bases in multiple countries were scheduled to meet at a hotel not far from Frankfurt, Germany, for an annual conference sponsored by the Protestant Women of the Chapel in Europe. I was to be their keynote speaker, which meant delivering five keynote messages and two workshops. The conference lasted five days, and including travel days we would be out of the country for eight days.

The decision about whether or not to go was very complicated. I had marked out two weekends on the calendar before and after this conference because of the long travel and the jetlag this assignment would involve. Also, the honorarium for this event was larger than my usual fee because the conference was considerably longer in duration than most women's events in the States.

Gene and I agonized over whether we could leave the country with so much at stake for our son, but we were acutely aware that the group was counting on my participation — and the honorarium would fully cover our next installment on Jason's monumental legal fees. After checking with our son's attorney, we were assured there was nothing we could do stateside to help with the preparation for J.P.'s trial during that time period. Bill Barnett encouraged us to go.

It was a long flight across the Atlantic Ocean, and I thought about who was going to be in the audience — young military wives, much like my daughter-in-law, April — except their husbands were actively serving our country in various divisions of the armed services, and my son, a young lieutenant in the Navy, was incarcerated. In the middle of the flight I began to weep. First, a Kleenex was enough to catch the tears. But then my weeping turned to sobbing, and I buried my head in my husband's chest. We both knew this would be a very difficult ministry assignment. These people were doing what my son longed to do — serve his country through military service. And that type of an assignment would probably never again be part of his future.

After going through customs, we slapped on smiles and warmly greeted the animated people who met us at the airport. The drive to Willigen, Germany, from Frankfurt was picturesque. Once we arrived at the hotel, the lobby was alive with excitement as the women began registering. They had traveled from U.S. military bases in France, Great Britain, Spain, Belgium, Italy, and, of course, Germany. Some arranged to come to the conference via military transport planes. Others drove to the conference. A few groups chartered buses.

When one of the busloads arrived, the women were exuberant. Their bus had broken down in a remote area, and instead of griping and complaining about the delay, the women sang songs of praise and worship while they waited for the missing parts to arrive. When the women ran out of songs to sing, they started taking turns sharing their personal stories of how Jesus Christ had transformed their lives. Before the missing parts arrived, these women led their bus driver to Christ.

During one of the first sessions in this multiple-day conference, one of the other speakers was introduced. Rhonda Miller, Director of Volunteers for Prison Fellowship, asked everyone in the audience to stand. Then she had half of them sit down. Looking at those left standing, she said, "You represent the percentage of inmates who can read." Then she asked all but the conference committee to sit down, leaving less than ten women on their feet. "You represent the percentage of inmates who had a loving father." Gene and I looked at each other and tears ran down our cheeks as we realized what a small minority our son was in — incarcerated with a university education and a loving father and mother.

As each day followed another, it was obvious that God's anointing was on this conference. The women were celebrating their faith as sisters in Christ, enthusiastically engaging in worship, and laughing and crying during the main sessions and in their small groups. God's Spirit was moving in a powerful way as truth was spoken and hearts were transformed.

In addition to the keynote sessions, I had volunteered to do a workshop called "I Have a Story to Tell," which focused on how to share your faith with others. When I arrived at the meeting room, it was filled to capacity and there were women sitting on all of the chairs; they were seated on tables in the back of the room; they were seated on the floor at the sides and in the front of the room. The participants had no idea how broken I was emotionally. As I witnessed their eagerness to hear what I had to say, I sensed that God was sending me a timely and vital message. "Carol," He whispered to my heart, "I'm not through with you yet. You have a job to do, and there are many spiritually needy women just like these women all over the world. Continue to do what I've called you to do. I can work much more effectively through your broken spirit than I could through your former professionalism and self-confidence. Trust Me."

I spent the next hour explaining how to put their personal testimony together, so they could share their story of how they began a walk of faith with Christ. When I got to the part about what to include in the prayer when someone wants to become a Christian, I saw several blank stares and I realized some of these women who came to a workshop on how to share their faith had never made the personal choice to follow Jesus themselves. I said, "Perhaps some of you would like to pray this prayer today." That afternoon seven young military wives invited Jesus into their lives — and they began sharing their decision with women from their own military bases.

God was moving in hearts. Women were coming to Christ. There was confession of sin. There was brokenness and restoration. What I thought would be the most difficult experience of my public speaking career turned out to be one of the most encouraging and uplifting opportunities of my life. My heart was hurting and my eyes were sore from weeping, but being with 500 women who were separated from their husbands and their mamas and their sisters and their stateside friends, women who were eager to hear God's truth and attend an English-speaking conference, was surprisingly renewing and refreshing.

In Germany I discovered the truth of the psalmist's words: "Those who sow in tears will reap with songs of joy. Those who go out weeping, carrying seed to sow, will return with songs of joy, carrying sheaves with them."[14] God used the brokenness of my heart to allow me to minister to those military wives with genuine compassion and with a spiritual empowerment that can only be explained in the supernatural dimension. It was a strange paradox to feel the grave sadness for our son's circumstances, while at the same time celebrating the moving of God's Spirit at this conference.

PRIVATE ANGUISH

On the fourth day of the event Gene and I finally had an evening to ourselves. We had been able to get a few calls through to our daughter-in-law and to our office. Nothing had changed regarding J.P.'s situation. We knew he was still healing from the wounds inflicted during the beating, but we believed he was safer now because he had finally been moved, at his written request soon after his incarceration, to the faith-based area of the maximum-security portion of the Orange County Jail. This was a major answer to my prayers, as this cell area is known for being less violent than the general population areas. The accommodations, food, and restrictions are the same, but Christian speakers held regular chapel services, and there was potential for Jason to have fellowship with other spiritually based inmates who had also requested the faith-based atmosphere. Jason was twice elected, by a vote of his peers, to be the Cell Coordinator in the faith-based area. His job was to help keep the peace, to enforce the guidelines in the faith-based block, and to work with the chaplain as chapel programs were brought in. I couldn't help but flash back in my mind to a few years earlier when he was elected president of the National Honor Society in high school. So many things had changed, but I was encouraged to know that God was evidently still using the leadership ability He'd built within our son to positively impact the lives of others.

Gene and I had dinner downstairs in the ballroom with the other conference participants and went back to our room early. We fell into bed that night exhausted. I felt Gene's hand touch my leg. Then he moved in closely and began curving his body to the shape of mine. He gently slid his hand over my arm, my shoulder, my neck, and my back. I warmed to his touch and sensed his need for me, but I felt a strange emotion. We had not made love since that fateful call brought shock, agony, and uncertainty crashing into our lives. The thought of doing something pleasurable when our son was locked up, accused of first-degree murder with the death penalty hanging over his head, seemed unthinkable to me.

Gene and I didn't speak. We sensed each other's confliction over the issue of sexual intimacy. My patient husband held me tenderly for a long time. I felt his tears against my cheek, and found safety, connection, and peace in his strong embrace. Slowly, our bodies began to move with the rhythm of deep love, built on many years of the shared experience of bringing pleasure to the other. The sweetness of the moment was filled with unspeakable appreciation for each other. Then, without warning, we both burst into tears and wept uncontrollably. In that tender and passionate moment we realized with a searing pain that cut to our core that the kind of precious married love we had just experienced might never be shared between Jason and April again.

In his journal Gene wrote about those emotion-packed moments:

> Last night Carol and I touched each other to comfort one another
> and ended in consummate passion and tears. Hot, broken tears of
> pain endured, of dreams lost — for ourselves, for our son and his wife
> and children. A lost future that cannot be reclaimed. A life that will
> never be as it once was. No matter what the legal outcome is, life will
> never be the same. Tears flooded over our faces and mingled together.
> Tears of frustration. Tears of love toward one another. Tears of
> pain unspeakable. We know we will survive. Life will go on . . . but we
> wouldn't mind having Jesus come back soon.

THE POWER *of* HEARTACHE

Our unexpected journey acquainted me quickly with a new range of emotion. Suddenly I found that my heart was more tender, my compassion for the needs of others was magnified, and my ability to weep with those who had hard lives or difficult personal situations was deepened.

Tears are powerful. They give us an outlet when we think we will burst with pain, hurt, betrayal, loneliness, loss, or disappointment. They provide comfort for those who need someone to weep with them. Most important, the tears of sorrow and heartbreak matter intimately to the heart of God. "You've kept track of my every toss and turn through the sleepless nights," the psalmist wrote. "Each tear entered in your ledger, each ache written in your book."[15]

Heartache is not a state of emotion that any of us want to experience. But none of us get off this planet without feeling deep woundedness to one degree or another. The "benefit," I have discovered, is very bittersweet. Author Ken Gire expresses my experience so well:

> The closest communion with God comes, I believe, through the sacrament of tears. Just as grapes are crushed to make wine and grain to make bread, so the elements of this sacrament come from the crushing experiences of life.[16]

The psalmist concurs: "The LORD is close to the brokenhearted and saves those who are crushed in spirit."[17]

The "crushing" was relentless as I grieved over my son, but one day a few months later I truly thought my heart would break apart, permanently, inside my chest. The spring of 2000 came to Michigan slowly. Patches of snow were still visible in early April. It even seemed like the daffodils and tulips were having an unusually hard time proving a season change was around the corner. I found myself welcoming the gray, rainy days that eventually brought us to May. The heaviness of the weather matched the atmosphere in my heart and gave me nonverbal permission to cry.

These depressing feelings came to a head on Mother's Day. We went to church, forgetting about the flowers the ushers passed out to honor all of the mothers at the end of the service. The bright red carnation in my hand was a vivid reminder that I had failed as a mother, that my son had committed a heinous crime, and that I would not be sharing a meal with my only child and his family on this special day.

Gene did his best to buffer the pain by trying to take me out for a meal at our favorite restaurant, but I refused. I tried to explain that being around other families that were celebrating such a significant day would only increase the hurt and possibly bring on a puddle of emotions in a public place. I just wanted to go home.

For hours I waited for the phone to ring. I just needed to hear from my son, to know he was okay, and to have a verbal connection. The call never came. I knew all of his days of incarceration were melting into one day that kept repeating itself over and over again. I doubted he even knew it was Mother's Day. My tears began slowly and then became unstoppable.

Walking over to the sofa, I picked up the light beige afghan my mother had crocheted for me several years earlier. It had arrived with a note in her distinctive handwriting: "Dear Carol, I prayed for you with every stitch. Love, Mother." Mom had made it extra large so it could be used as a blanket when we had overnight guests, or as a comfy lap blanket on a cold day. It was precious to me and I always folded it in an attractive way and displayed it in a prominent place.

That afternoon I opened the afghan to its largest dimensions and hunkered down inside the soft folds, encircling my body with the treasured gift from my neck to my toes. It felt good to cry hard on Mother's Day wrapped inside something my mother had made with her own hands. In the middle of my deep sadness, I started to talk out loud to God. "Father, I am so broken, hurting, and totally unable to find peace on this day when other mothers are hugging their children and hearing words of affirmation and thanks. I am ashamed of my inability to cope with this sorrow. I see the agony on Gene's face. He doesn't know how to help me, and it hurts me even more to see him trying to find a way to comfort me when I don't want to be comforted. I just want to quit living. I am weary of this pain that never goes away. Please rescue me. And if You do not remove me from this place of hurt, will You please climb inside this afghan with me and hold me? What do You want me to see? To learn? I am listening. Do You have anything to tell me?"

Instinctively, I reached for my Bible and turned to a passage my mother often quoted from memory when I was growing up, Psalm 91. On that day of so much grieving, God spoke to me, this time from *The Message*:

> You who sit down in the High God's presence, spend the night in Shaddai's shadow, Say this: "GOD, you're my refuge. I trust in you and I'm safe!"
>
> "If you'll hold on to me for dear life," says GOD, "I'll get you out of any trouble. I'll give you the best of care if you'll only get to know and trust me. Call me and I'll answer, be at your side in bad times; I'll rescue you."[18]

I turned back a few pages and read:

I learned God-worship when my pride was shattered. Heart-shattered lives ready for love don't for a moment escape God's notice.[19]

I had a quiet knowing deep inside my heart. As I pulled Mama's afghan more snuggly around my body, I realized I was being hugged by the God who loved me. I was learning about the power of worship in a dark valley. I spoke aloud to God, "Father, I open my hands and ask You to guide me through these uncharted waters. Please fill the hole in my heart. Your presence is sweeter than I've ever known before. I hate this process, but I do love You in a different and more all-consuming way. I know something about You and me is different and better. I hate the reason why this deeper intimacy is being birthed. But I embrace the sweetness and I love You."

My Isaac experience was a crisis that came into my life without announcement and without warning. I didn't choose to be a Christian "martyr," and I didn't ask to take this situation on as "my cross to bear." It was plunged like a spear into my heart. Ever since I have had to decide, day by day, how to respond to it. One way has been with the relief valve of human tears. Pouring out my heartache to God has brought me into His comforting embrace in a way I could never have imagined. I am no longer ashamed or embarrassed when someone sees me sad or weeping. It gives me an opportunity to remind them (and myself) that there is a day coming when "God will wipe every last tear from [our] eyes."[20]

Laying our Isaac down is the hardest decision we will ever have to make. It feels risky, awkward, impractical, frightening, and ridiculous. But our heart knows it's the right thing to do. We bow in worship before the God who loves us more than we love our Isaac and opens our fists. And in the process of releasing, we find ourselves deeply loved. The love is born from within Him, not from what He sees in us. That's a good thing, because we know we're not worth all that much. But in His eyes, we are worth everything. He has already shown us how much. He gave the greatest heart sacrifice known to man — His only son.

God's Power in *Your* Circumstances

Genesis 22 does not record any tears from Abraham. We do know that Abraham and Isaac traveled toward the place of sacrifice for three days, so I can't help but wonder about the many emotions that must have filled this father's heart as he made the most challenging journey of his life. The Bible is full of stories of people like Abraham — like you and me — who were asked by God to be faithful in the midst of crushing circumstances. I don't know about you, but I find comfort in the fact that most of them did not get an answer to their *why?* questions either. Heartache is a common denominator among human beings, and I draw strength from knowing I am not as alone as I sometimes feel.

1. How have you typically dealt with heartache in the past? For example, have you cried easily or have you avoided crying? Do you find crying helpful, embarrassing, both? Reflect on why you do what you do with your sadness.

2. Have you experienced the timely presence of a "comforting companion," as I did when my friend Cathy Gallagher "showed up" for me in a powerful and unforgettable way? If so, make a point to write a note of thanks to this "angel" God sent your way. Think of someone you know who is currently experiencing heartache. How might you "show up" for this person as a comforting companion, even from a distance? (Be creative!)

3. When was the last time you wondered, *Why didn't God do something?* Make a list of all the thoughts and emotions you experienced (or are now experiencing) while in the wilderness of *why?*

4. Recall a time when God used the brokenness of your heart to enable you to minister to someone else in a meaningful way — big or small. How did that experience serve to give you a different perspective on your own heartache?

5. Do you agree with Ken Gire's statement, "The closest communion with God comes, I believe, through the sacrament of tears"? How have you experienced this most recently? Ask God to reveal fresh

mysteries to you regarding the power of worship in your darkest valleys.

6. If you are encountering heartache over a current Isaac experience, consider praying out loud to God, as I did, pouring out your raw and uncensored thoughts, feelings, hopes, and fears. Allow God into the crushed places inside you and ask Him to embrace you with a comfort beyond anything you've experienced before. (If you're not practiced at this level of intimate communion with God, give it time and repeat your heartfelt prayers often!)

$\mathcal{S}$TRETCHER BEARERS AND YELLOW ROSES

The Power *of* Community

*A friend hears the song in my heart
and sings it to me when my memory fails.*
—ANONYMOUS

WE WERE LIVING IN A GRIEF THAT NEVER ENDED AS PEOPLE from around the country continued to contact us. Cards and letters flooded our mailbox.

I discovered a daily rhythm in my grieving. When the sunshine was bright and the day was young, I was able to cope with the sadness. But as late afternoon would lessen the amount of natural light coming in the windows, dusk would soon appear and I started struggling with hopelessness and depression. I often positioned myself near the phone, waiting endlessly for calls to come from my son and hoping for any positive word from the attorney.

The cloud of depression was already descending on me in the first week of our journey, when one afternoon the doorbell rang. Gene had left for a meeting and I was home alone. The doorbell rang a second time and I headed for the front door. Peeking through a side window, I could tell it was the florist attempting to make a delivery. I opened the door and there stood the delivery-man with a large object in his hand. It was covered with florist paper. He smiled widely and asked, "Are you Carol Kent?"

I nodded and he continued. "Well, Ma'am, it's your lucky day! Somebody must want to make you feel special today, and I have the privilege of delivering this gift. Enjoy your day!"

It was a day when his cheery greeting wasn't at all what I desired. My first response was to tell him to go find someone else to shower his joy on, but my well-mannered, first-born-preacher's-kid training kicked into gear. I received the gift with as much graciousness as I could muster, mumbled, "Thank you," and carried the covered object to my kitchen. Tearing away the protective covering, my eyes fell on one dozen of the most perfect long-stemmed yellow roses I had ever seen. At that very moment the clouds opened and a stream of sunshine came through my kitchen skylight and landed on that exquisite yellow bouquet.

I wondered who knew I was having a particularly bad day and might need a message of hope. Opening the envelope, my eyes fell on these words:

Dear Carol,
You once gave us some decorating advice that was very helpful. You said, "Yellow flowers will brighten any room." We thought you could use a little yellow in your life right now.
> Love,
> Bonnie & Joy

The note was from two of my sisters. I burst into tears and sobbed like a baby. As I gazed at the flowers, I realized I wasn't alone in this long vigil of waiting on what would happen next. My sisters and many others were waiting with us, and they were trying their best to let us know we were not alone.

From that point on, yellow became my color of sunshine and hope. Word spread quickly, and yellow cards started arriving in my mailbox. People sent yellow candles, yellow coffee cups, and packages wrapped in yellow paper. The gift of yellow roses ignited a whole community of friends and family who began networking with each other to provide encouragement, compassion, and acts of kindness toward our family.

STRETCHER BEARERS

Several months into our journey I received an e-mail from a friend in Arizona. She told me she felt the Lord was leading her to network our friends together in a way that could provide physical, emotional, and monetary help during this devastating time. Her name was Kathe Wunnenberg. Within two weeks another note came from Becky Freeman, a friend from Texas, expressing the same desire to help. These two women had never met each other, but their requests were identical.

It was hard for Gene and me to consider accepting such an offer. We were used to being on the giving end of compassion and mercy. It was a huge step for us to acknowledge that perhaps this was God's way of helping to meet the needs of our family during the long months of waiting for Jason's trial. We connected Kathe and Becky with each other and before long, these two wonder women launched a monthly update letter to people who wanted to be a part of encouraging our family.

Kathe dubbed the group Stretcher Bearers. Several years before she had heard a pastor, Michael Slater, speak about his book *Becoming a Stretcher Bearer*,[1] which encourages people to put "feet" to their prayers through active encouragement. Pastor Slater was launching a ministry based on the apostle Mark's dramatic account about the compassionate and inventive band of friends who came to the rescue of a paralyzed man by carrying him on a stretcher so he could get to Jesus for healing. The same story is told in Luke 5:17-26.

> One day as he was teaching, Pharisees and religion teachers were sitting around. They had come from nearly every village in Galilee and Judea, even as far away as Jerusalem, to be there. The healing power of God was on him.
>
> Some men arrived carrying a paraplegic on a stretcher. They were looking for a way to get into the house and set him before Jesus. When they couldn't find a way in because of the crowd, they went up on the roof, removed some tiles, and let him down in the middle of everyone, right in front of Jesus. Impressed by their bold

belief, he said, "Friend, I forgive your sins."

That set the religion scholars and Pharisees buzzing. "Who does he think he is? That's blasphemous talk! God and only God can forgive sins."

Jesus knew exactly what they were thinking and said, "Why all this gossipy whispering? Which is simpler: to say 'I forgive your sins,' or to say 'Get up and start walking'? Well, just so it's clear that I'm the Son of Man and authorized to do either, or both...." He now spoke directly to the paraplegic: "Get up. Take your bedroll and go home." Without a moment's hesitation, he did it—got up, took his blanket, and left for home, giving glory to God all the way. The people rubbed their eyes, incredulous—and then also gave glory to God. Awestruck, they said, "We've never seen anything like that!"[2]

In this story about one of the miracles Jesus performed, there are specific, fundamental factors that make the account intriguing and instructive:

- An individual needed help, and in his paralyzed state, he couldn't get the assistance he needed by himself.
- He had friends who saw his need.
- These friends interrupted their personal agendas and got involved in giving tangible help to someone else.
- They physically carried their friend when he couldn't carry himself.
- They faced a big obstacle. The crowd was so huge that they couldn't walk their friend in the door and get close enough to get Jesus' personal attention.
- The friends got creative. They carried their helpless friend on his stretcher up to the rooftop. They made an opening and lowered their friend to Jesus through the ceiling.
- Once the friends got the man to Jesus, He forgave the man's sins and healed him.
- The man got up and walked, picked up his bedroll, praised God, and left for home.

- Jesus turned the miracle into a teachable moment for the crowd.
- People were "awestruck" and said they had never seen anything like this before.

Our Stretcher Bearers were not unlike those described in the gospel passage above. They were friends who recognized that we were in need, and they decided to take action. Kathe and Becky got together, along with Kathy Blume, my dear friend who was already in charge of my team of ministry intercessors, and they launched the largest campaign I've ever seen to inform our friends across the country about how they could assist our family during the challenging months ahead.

They sent out specific lists of key players who would be involved in the court case, and hundreds of people began praying by name for Judge Fred Lauten, and for attorneys Bill Barnett and Bert Barclay. They prayed for the prosecutor, Dorothy Sedgwick, and for the psychiatrists who would be interviewing J.P. They faithfully prayed for the family of Douglas Miller Jr. They prayed for Jason, April, and for Chelsea and Hannah. And, of course, they also covered Gene and me with prayer.

We knew it would be challenging for April to continue homeschooling her daughters during the time of the trial, so the Stretcher Bearers covered the cost of sending the girls to a Christian school. They sent out reminders when Jason, April, and the girls had birthdays and special events. When they discovered that April's favorite color was purple, she started receiving purple paper-ware, purple candles, purple cards, and purple-wrapped surprises. Chelsea and Hannah were showered with books, tapes, CDs, and stuffed animals. Gifts of encouragement arrived almost daily.

They also wrote letters and sent cards to J.P. One of the few things that can be sent to a jail or prison besides a letter is a book, and Jason was sent many helpful and uplifting books that he read personally and then recycled through countless other men who were incarcerated with him.

We were now seeing J.P. in the regular visiting area, not in the "special visit" room where there were telephones so you could easily hear each other talk. In the regular visiting area there was a line of cubicles right next to each other, with up to five people crowding into each small, filthy area that had only one chair. The window was lined with an aluminum frame that had holes in it. The only way to communicate with your family member was to speak (talk loudly, yell, or scream) into the holes, with everyone on both sides doing the same thing. On my sister Jennie's first visit, she looked to the cubicle on the right and saw a baby who was less than a week old being held by a teenage mother. The young woman was screaming to the man on the other side of the glass, "This is too your baby! You better believe this is your baby!"

During each Saturday night visit we were able to participate in, we made a feeble attempt at cleaning the thick windowpane that separated us from our son. We were not allowed to have physical contact — no hugs, no holding hands while we prayed for each other, no embraces between J.P. and his wife and stepdaughters. "Touching through glass" was our best connection. We held our hands up to the glass, and J.P. did the best he could to "touch" us, but because he was in handcuffs, chained to his waist, it was a painful stretch for him to touch the glass very often.

BEARING *each* OTHER'S BURDENS

By today's standards I'm from a big family. I had always enjoyed our joy-filled Sunday dinners around Mother and Dad's big dining room table. It seemed that our family always planned for enough food so we could invite extra people home from church with us. Mom would feed them and Dad would give them biblical counsel. Our parents worked like a hand in a glove in the ministry together. Mom and Dad taught me "the power of community" long before I desperately needed the compassion and comfort of a supportive group of people in order to survive our ordeal.

When our tragedy struck, it had never occurred to me that being from a large family would be such a blessing. My four sisters and my brother had always showered Gene and me with love, and they also dearly loved our son. Now I got to see just how much.

Jennie, the sister next to me in the birth order, was in deep grief. On the fourth day following Jason's arrest, she wrote: "I've been tossing and turning since 4:00 A.M. and finally got up to study and pray. I love you. Sometimes I feel your pain so keenly I'm overwhelmed with it."

Paula, next in birth order and six years my junior, wrote to Jason within days of the incident:

> Dear J.P.,
>
> I am so filled with love for you that words cannot express. My thoughts and prayers are with you all through the days and nights. I hurt for you. I cry for you. I thank God for you and for the example you have been for my own son and for many others. I don't understand what it is God would have us learn from this situation. I know God is faithful and Jesus never fails. I not only believe in miracles, I expect and am waiting to witness one.

Bonnie, the fourth daughter born to our family, instantly came alongside our mother and father, helping them to get through the emotions of the first couple of weeks. Bonnie would often call me as the light of day was turning to dusk, because she knew that was the time of day when I struggled the most.

My only brother, Ben, is a Deputy U.S. Marshall in Washington, D.C. He is a lot like Jason in his fierce determination to stand up for the underdog and to rescue anyone in danger. Ben called regularly to assure me that J.P. would be okay. Ben also spoke of something I didn't want to hear, suggesting that God's next ministry for J.P., for the foreseeable future, would be to teach the Word to men behind bars.

My youngest sister, Joy, wrote with her usual authenticity as the first week of the crisis was ending.

> Hi Carol,
>
> I just wanted you to know that the black cloud is lifting off our house. Today was the first day I was able to sing and pray — really pray. I still bawl through my quiet time, but the heaviness is more

bearable. We're in this together . . . I love you so much. I hope it helps to know we share your pain.

I had experienced being in a family with five siblings for many years, but in the middle of my time of greatest need I discovered what real "community" is and how God designed people — through the relatives and the friends in my life — to help me experience the unconditional love and compassion of Jesus. It was the worst of times, but it was the best of times. I was hurting badly, but I was being loved deeply.

As month followed month, I had better days, but I also had some very bad days. There had already been two postponements of the trial, and the days and months were dragging by with our son still incarcerated in the county jail. Limbo.

It was October 24, 2000, twelve months after Jason's arrest. A year earlier we had been looking forward to his illustrious future as a naval officer with his first assignment in Honolulu. We anticipated family reunions in a tropical paradise. All of our reunions were now held at the jail. The legal process was so slow, it didn't even feel like it was crawling.

On this "anniversary" of the incident that changed our lives, I could feel myself sliding fast into depression. It seemed there was little to no hope that there would be a positive outcome. My heart was breaking for my son. I spent much of that day weeping, looking at family scrapbooks from happier years, and allowing myself to sink into the depths of my grief. Nighttime finally allowed me to escape into sleep.

The following morning I awoke and my unbearable heaviness was strangely gone. I felt fresh hope. It was as if someone had lifted the weight of sorrow off my shoulders and freed me to experience a normal day. I had a surprising sense of optimism. The change was dramatic.

Later, I received a copy of this journal entry, written on her computer by my sister Bonnie:

It was October 25, 2000, my husband Ron's fiftieth birthday. I usually make birthdays a celebration for the person who has made it

through another year. However, on this memorable day for my husband, I woke up feeling deep sadness.

One year earlier, our family had gone through the pain of receiving a call telling us that my nephew, Jason, had shot and killed a man, believing the he was protecting his stepdaughters from potential abuse. Yet, here I was, twelve months later, in severe pain. I could barely catch my breath. The grief was beyond understanding.

At noon I broke down and called Carol, hoping to gain some relief, but when I heard her voice, I burst into tears. No words would come. I don't know how she figured out who it was through my sobbing, but I know she thanked me for my tears.

That night I took my husband out for a birthday dinner celebration at our favorite restaurant, and once again I broke down and wept. I tried to explain to him that I couldn't understand what was happening to me, but it was as if J.P. was my own son.

When I read about Bonnie's experience, God brought a Scripture to my mind that I'd memorized years before: "Carry each other's burdens, and in this way you will fulfill the law of Christ."[3] I had an instant realization that God had allowed my sister to carry the load of grief in my heart for one day. He allowed her to be my "burden-bearer" because I was bowing under the load and needed a break from the sorrow. Bonnie and I instinctively knew it was a spiritual experience, far different from anything we had known before. Preacher and master storyteller Jess Moody describes it poignantly:

Did you ever take a *real* trip down inside the broken heart of a friend? To feel the sob of the soul — the raw, red crucible of emotional agony? To have this become almost as much yours as that of your soul-crushed neighbor? Then, to sit down with him — and silently weep? This is the beginning of compassion.[4]

I used to think I was a compassionate person who cared for the needs of others. After all, I felt sorry for people who had problems and challenges in their lives. I even shed an occasional tear for the difficulties of others. However, until I found myself flat-out needy, I never understood what the power of community could do. It's people in the body of Christ working like a family to sit and cry with you. Holding you. Caring for your needs. Carrying your burden for a day. Creatively solving problems. Gathering resources. Opening doors of hope. Writing notes of encouragement. Fighting a cause on your behalf. Finding a way when there is no way. Listening. Waiting with you as long as it takes. It's people "being Jesus" to you.

The longer Gene and I have experienced what it is to be needy — emotionally, spiritually, and financially — the more personally we have comprehended what it means to be cared for by the body of Christ. The word "care" is both a noun and a verb. It involves not only *feeling* interest or concern, but also actively *giving care*, up close and personal. The dictionary describes active caring as "painstaking or watchful attention." The apostle Paul put it this way:

> If you've gotten anything at all out of following Christ, if his love has made any difference in your life, if being in a community of the Spirit means anything to you, if you have a heart, if you *care*—then do me a favor: Agree with each other, love each other, be deep-spirited friends. Don't push your way to the front; don't sweet-talk your way to the top. Put yourself aside, and help others get ahead. Don't be obsessed with getting your own advantage. Forget yourselves long enough to lend a helping hand.[5]

I have been continually awestruck by all the efforts of our relatives and friends to *care* in every tangible way imaginable, as well as to heed Paul's similar but simple admonition to the Philippians: "Help needy Christians; be inventive in hospitality."[6]

One of God's richest "pick-me-ups" took place at the Christian Booksellers' Association Convention several months after Jason's arrest. I had lunch with about thirty-five friends who are also speakers and authors. Many of us live far from each other, but we have become close friends due to our mutual interest in speaking and writing ministries. After I briefly shared the story of our journey with the group, my dear friend Kim Moore led us in worship, singing "Shout to the Lord." I cried through the entire song. Then my Christian sisters encircled me, laid hands on me, wept, and prayed for our family. It was one of the most tender experiences of my life — being comforted and prayed over by friends who were helping to carry our burden. As we finished, we were on our knees; some of my friends were prostrate before the Lord. It was a holy experience that I will never forget.

A FELLOWSHIP *like* NO OTHER

My friend Tom has experienced the literal life-saving power of community in a whole different context than I have known. Here is his story, in his own words:

> Looking back on my life, I realize I have made some of my most life-changing decisions on Sundays. Sunday, August 16, 1991, was no exception. I was lounging on my deck, cooking in the late afternoon sun. In one hand I held a cigarette, in the other a tall glass of the driest Chardonnay I could afford. I needed nothing else. And that's the way I liked it.
>
> I had met Jesus fifteen years before, on a Sunday, when I was a preteen. At that time I had never touched liquor. I gave my life to Christ right before I reached the age when temptations to experiment with alcohol and drugs would begin to abound. While I had plenty of other personal challenges during my adolescent years, getting caught up with "the wrong crowd" wasn't one of them. Almost all my friends were believers, and I practically lived at church. I loved it there. I felt safe. At home the liquor flowed, and I wanted nothing to do with it. Through the years I had watched my father's downward spiral. To this day my most vivid memory of him is his hands — a cigarette in one and a martini in the other, holding the edges of the evening newspaper that obscured him completely from waist to head. He rarely looked at me, but I stared at the backside of his newspaper a lot as puffs of smoke swirled around the room and the sound of ice

tinkled in his glass. Remote. Inaccessible. Silent. That was my father.

Now, two decades later, here I was in the hot August sun, knocking back my third glass of wine and wanting nothing but more of the same. A "Do not disturb" sign hung invisibly over my head, just as it had over my father's. People had learned to leave me alone. My phone rarely rang anymore. Certainly no one stopped by. And that's the way I liked it.

Or was it? I had been living this way for a while now. When I first discovered the power alcohol had to make me feel "okay" in my own skin, I was in my midtwenties. I hated the taste of the stuff in the beginning, but I *loved* the way it made me feel. And I loved the social life that almost magically sprung up around it. I had gotten away from going to church since moving to a new city. The familiar loneliness of my childhood settled in around me like a gray cloud. When I started accepting invitations to happy hour with some coworkers, I felt like my "real life" had finally begun. I had lots of friends, lots of parties, lots of fun.

When had it all changed? How did I get here — alone every weekend, every evening — making love to my bottle?

I hauled myself up to refill my glass. Emptying what little was left in the bottle on the kitchen counter, I turned to the refrigerator where an unopened jug was waiting. As I stared into the refrigerator my heart started to race. *Where was the bottle?* It wasn't there. I looked in the garage, in my car. Nothing. Panic rising, I raced to the linen closet in the bathroom where I usually kept a stash. Nothing. *How could I have let this happen?* It was Sunday. The liquor stores were closed. I was always so careful to check my supply on Saturdays so nothing like this would ever happen.

My mind had accelerated to full gallop. *What should I do?* I liked to drink alone. That was the whole point. I didn't want to go out to some noisy bar on a Sunday night. *Were the bars even open on Sunday?* I had no idea. I had spent so many weekends holed up with my private stash that I didn't even know where I could buy booze in an emergency.

I stared at the empty bottle on the counter. I couldn't believe my eyes, my fate. Alone on a Sunday evening with *nothing*. I thought I needed nothing. But I *needed* a bottle. And suddenly I didn't like it that way.

My "moment of truth" had arrived, completely uninvited. I don't remember anything else about that night. I know I didn't leave the house. I didn't replenish my supply. My next memory is of 5:00 P.M. the next day, when I buckled up in my car after my normal Monday. I had felt okay today. After all, I wasn't one of those poor sops who had to take some pops during the day. My drinking was within perfectly sane boundaries. *I* decided when I drank, and I could always wait until at least 5:20.

That was only twenty minutes from now. I froze. I couldn't start the car. I couldn't go home to no booze, but I couldn't go to the liquor store either. Something was stopping me, like one of those angels I'd read about in the Bible who was barring the way with a flaming sword. I sat behind the wheel of my car and shook with terror. *What in the world was wrong with me?*

I did go home eventually. I didn't go to the liquor store. I don't remember what I did. All I can recall now is an evening of being trampled by what the "Big Book" of Alcoholics Anonymous refers to as "the hideous Four Horsemen — Terror, Bewilderment, Frustration, Despair."[7]

By 5:00 P.M. the next day I was truly desperate. Before leaving the office I looked up the number for Alcoholics Anonymous in the phone book and made the call to "those people" I had heard of but never dreamed in my worst nightmares I would need. I didn't know what I needed — except a drink. I didn't want to need anything else. I had liked it that way.

Almost thirteen years have passed since I walked into my first meeting of Alcoholics Anonymous. I fully expected to hate it, hate "them," and never come back. But they — a kind, generous, affable, perfectly "normal" looking crowd of recovering drunks — told me to "keep coming back." I did. I was shocked to meet so many people of faith in the rooms. I soon learned that their path to sobriety and serenity was fundamentally spiritual. Everyone credited God with the miracles we witnessed day after day — and now year after year. I am one of those miracles.

I understand my father now, as I understand myself. Alcoholism, I have learned, is fundamentally a disease of isolation. I have yet to meet an alcoholic — drunk or sober — who doesn't count self-reliance and loneliness in their top five "symptoms," and this is true whether we overtly withdraw from others or are the "life of the party." Our Twelve-Step program text affirms that "our liquor was but a symptom"[8] of a complex and devastating sickness of mind, body, and soul.

As I continue to recover, one day at a time, from the family disease of alcoholism, I enjoy a richer fellowship with other human beings than I ever dreamed possible. I'm never home on Sunday nights now. I'm at my favorite AA meeting with some of the most wonderful and supportive people I've ever met. And I like it that way.

THE POWER *of* COMMUNITY

We never know how desperately we need people in our lives until an Isaac experience forces us to admit, first to ourselves and then to others, that we can't make it alone. Karen Burton Mains refers to this community of helpers as her "holders." She writes,

> Holders are people who stand beside us even when things are unpleasant; they have a capacity to stay unshaken for the long haul. . . . Holders are not afraid to speak the truth. . . . Truth simply spoken can be one of the greatest comforts. . . . I've come to realize that the people who help me the most are the ones who have the questions, not the ones who have the answers.[9]

Gene and I began to see a pattern among those who grieved with us. Initially, people were in shock and had a need to "do something." As we got past the two-month point of their initial knowledge of our crisis, our "holders," who were beside us for the long haul, were the people who "stuck like glue" and refused to let us withdraw from society and relationship.

As I've been writing this book, I've realized that due to my work as a traveling speaker, God opened a nationwide door of support for our family during this unthinkable crisis. There are, no doubt, many readers who can honestly say, "I don't have a network like that. Who is in my 'community of caring people'?" You might be an only child, or you might have a very small circle of friends. You may wonder if anybody really cares.

Soon after Gene and I received the devastating news that our son had pulled the trigger and killed a man, we went to the home of our pastor, Peter Foxwell, and his wife, Kim. They listened more than they talked. They comforted us by their presence. They didn't quote fifty Bible verses. Peter and Kim acknowledged our pain, hugged us, and prayed with us.

A trained Christian counselor, Kim asked, "Do you have any support people in your life?"

"Oh, yes," I said. "Even though the news has not been heard by everyone yet, we have had remarkable support."

Then she said something I will never forget: "When you're in a crisis, if you have only *one* supportive person, you can make it through the journey. We all need at least *one person* to be there for us in the middle of a tragedy."

Some time after that visit, a surprising and significant note came to us via the Stretcher Bearers who had sent updates to many of the people who knew our family personally. One of those update letters went to a former next-door neighbor. Our sons, J.P. and Chris, had been best friends in their growing up years. Tony wrote:

The Kents are among the nicest people I have ever met, so it stands to reason that April is very special also. As Gene and Carol would tell you, I am not a very religious or devout person, but I do believe in a

greater power and on occasion do pray to give thanks. I am sending a
check to April today. I do not know if I can be a Stretcher Bearer, but
I will carry the Band-aids.

Tony's note said it all. None of us can do *everything* for the people around us
who are in need. But all of us can do *something*. An interesting fact about stretch-
ers is that it is impossible for one person to carry a stretcher alone. It takes
the teamwork of several people working together to get the job done. In our
case, Tony was willing to carry the Band-aids by providing help toward April's
expenses, and others assisted with frequent-flyer miles for our trips to Florida.
Another friend made it her mission to send books to J.P. on a regular basis. The
primary assistance provided by others was prayer support. Some individuals
made personal encouragement to Chelsea and Hannah their "main thing." It
was a community of people who, one at a time, did what they knew they could
do — what the apostle Paul encouraged the early Christians to do.

> Those of us who are strong and able in the faith need to step in and
> lend a hand to those who falter, and not just do what is most conve-
> nient for us. Strength is for service, not status. Each one of us needs to
> look after the good of the people around us, asking ourselves, "How
> can I help?"
> That's exactly what Jesus did. He didn't make it easy for him-
> self by avoiding people's troubles, but waded right in and helped
> out. "I took on the troubles of the troubled," is the way Scripture
> puts it. Even if it was written in Scripture long ago, you can be sure
> it's written for *us*. God wants the combination of his steady, con-
> stant calling and warm, personal counsel in Scripture to come to
> characterize *us*, keeping us alert for whatever he will do next. May
> our dependably steady and warmly personal God develop maturity
> in you so that you get along with each other as well as Jesus gets
> along with us all. Then we'll be a choir — not our voices only, but
> our very lives singing in harmony in a stunning anthem to the God
> and Father of our Master Jesus!

So reach out and welcome one another to God's glory. Jesus did it; now you do it![10]

If you are a community of one and you see a need, you can still be a stretcher bearer. It starts with carrying the Band-aids.

God's Power in *Your* Circumstances

I have been a member of the body of Christ for more than forty-five years—most of my life. I have participated in more "networks" than I can count and am as "connected" socially and professionally as I can possibly be. However, until I was plunged into the devastation of my most difficult Isaac experience I never knew how much I had missed about the power of community. Sooner or later we will all end up on a stretcher due to the circumstances of life. The question is, who has God provided to lift us, and will we allow them to do it?

1. Are you more comfortable being on the giving or receiving end of active caring? Why? When was the last time you admitted that you cannot "make it" alone?

2. If you are currently having an Isaac experience, who knows about it? How much do they know? How much do you keep private, and why? Consider that Jesus might never have encountered, much less healed, the paralyzed man in Luke 5 if the man's friends had not first *seen*—and then responded to—his need. If your Isaac experience is in the category of heart sacrifices that involve difficult personal choices, your needs may not be immediately evident to those around you. What first step can you make to open the door to others who might help bear your burden?

3. I first learned about the power of community in my family of origin. In what contexts have you experienced the tangible support of others? Reflect on a time in your life when you could relate to what I wrote on page 82: "It was the worst of times, but it was the best of times. I was hurting badly, but I was being loved deeply." If you have not experienced this kind of love, why do you suppose that is?

4. Reflect on Jess Moody's description of true compassion on page 83. When was the last time you took a "*real* trip down inside the broken heart of a friend"? Get a pen and paper and try to capture in words or images what this experience was like for you and the person with whom you deeply empathized.

5. Who are your personal "holders"? Make a list of the people in this community of helpers and note some of the specific ways they have "been Jesus" to you.

6. I wrote on page 90: "None of us can do *everything* for the people around us who are in need. But all of us can do *something*." Just like the stretcher bearers who brought a paralyzed man to Jesus, it's people like you and me who make concrete choices to bear others' burdens. Identify someone in your current sphere of influence who needs some kind of assistance or encouragement. List the needs of this individual or family and consider what *you* could do to help meet one or more of these needs. How can you bring this person closer to Jesus — even if it means "going through the roof" by using an unusual method to accomplish your task? See how inventive you can be!

chapter five

*E*VEN IN THIS . . .

The Power *of* Hope

Our broken lives are not lost or useless. God's love is still working.
He comes in and takes the calamity and uses it victoriously,
working out his wonderful plan of love.
—ERIC LIDDELL

"WHY DIDN'T HE JUST SHOOT HIMSELF BEFORE HE GOT PICKED up by the police?" the woman asked. "It would have been a lot easier for everybody if he died, wouldn't it? If you were planning a funeral, there would be intense pain for a while, and then you could all begin healing. But in this situation, there's no end to the suffering, is there?"

I couldn't believe my ears. Was this woman, who called herself my friend, actually asking me those questions? Was she suggesting that just because our family had to face agonizing months of investigation, depositions, financial challenges, and visits to the jail, all resulting in an unknown future for Jason and for all of us, that it would be better if my son were *dead*? Was she suggesting that if a man goes to prison for several years, or even for the rest of his life, that his existence becomes *worthless*?

Did she know how hurtful her comments were to two parents who were already in unspeakable pain? *Was she an idiot, or was she simply an insensitive person? Did she really want me to respond to her questions? Did she think she was comforting us?*

One thing was certain. She didn't understand redemption.

Among the definitions of the word *redeem* is "to extricate from or help to overcome something detrimental"—even "to free from the consequences of sin." In my son's case, the consequences of his actions would no doubt be harsh and lifelong, but on a spiritual plane the effect of even the most heinous circumstances can be offset in miraculous ways that only a gracious and loving God can accomplish. In God's great salvage operation of redemption, something of value can be extracted from even the most putrid rubbish.

Most of us who have walked with Christ for a few years find it relatively easy to trust God for "the small stuff"—occasional financial reversals, minor physical challenges, relationship struggles, disappointments, lost opportunities. But an Isaac experience puts our relationship with God to the test. Do we *really* believe He is good and loving when our life is irrevocably altered in a way that causes hardship and heartache? When we experience a debilitating disease, accident, addiction, or heartbreaking loss due to another's choice or our own, will we still love, trust, obey, honor, and worship the God we've claimed to love, *even in this?* Even if nothing changes?

The "even in this" category of suffering makes the small stuff truly small, because what we have to deal with puts the rest of life into perspective. As we trust God to give us hearts to hope for and eyes to see redemption in the midst of an "even in this" situation, we can experience a spiritual and emotional empowerment that not only lifts our spirits, but also inspires people who are observing our response.

BEACONS *of* HOPE

Lisa Beamer never dreamed that the story of her husband, Todd, would reverberate around the world following the crash of United Flight 93 on September 11, 2001. Todd Beamer will go down in history as a 9-11 hero, and none of us will ever forget the recorded message of his now-famous words just before the plane crashed in a field in Pennsylvania: "Let's roll!" As I read Lisa's description of her pain, my heart resonated with her story:

For several weeks following September 11, I'd walk into Todd's closet, see his clothes, and start crying. Sometimes even now I go into the closet and close the doors. I crumple on the floor and, for a few minutes, just weep. I read the notes he wrote to me, touch his pillow, and wipe my tears with his T-shirt. I weep until there are no more tears, then take a deep breath, straighten myself up, and go back out to face whatever the day brings.

The tears still show up often in my life, sometimes when I least expect them . . . but that's what this earth is — happiness mixed with sadness.[1]

Lisa lived through the pain of an unexpected Isaac experience. She suddenly faced the death of her spouse, and she simultaneously dealt with the loss of the father of her two sons and her unborn daughter. She had to lay her Isaac down, but that didn't mean there would be no more pain or no more tears — not in *this* lifetime. Still, *even in this*, the Beamers' larger story of faith in unthinkable circumstances has been salvaged from the ashes and shared, to God's glory, with countless individuals around the globe.

Gracia (pronounced "*gray*-sha") Burnham and her husband, Martin, were roused out of bed one morning at gunpoint. Martin was a missionary pilot in the Philippines, and he and his wife were taken by the Abu Sayyaf terrorist group while celebrating their wedding anniversary at a resort. Following their kidnapping, they were held as captives for one year in the jungles of the Philippines, where they lived on the run without enough food, water, shelter, or warm clothing. They were chained to a tree each night and slept on the ground. Martin and Gracia had painful body sores and horrible intestinal viruses. Several of their fellow hostages were beheaded, and Martin was eventually shot and killed.

In the dramatic story of their year of horror and of Gracia's eventual release, she said:

Some people in America want me to be offended and angry and bitter with the government for not doing this or that. Others want me to be depressed and morose. . . . I can't be either of those. . . . What happened to Martin and me was no one's fault except that of sinful human beings, the kind we came to the Philippines to help. This ordeal went with the territory. I refuse to let this dampen my joy or detract from the love that God means to flourish in my heart. . . . I resolve to keep living in the embrace of God's gladness and love for as long as he gives me breath.[2]

Gracia Burnham laid her Isaac down. She could have chosen anger, bitterness, and hatred toward a group of terrorists who took her husband's life. She could have pointed fingers of accusation at the government for not coming to their rescue sooner. She could have stepped into a downward spiral of depression and despair. Instead, *even in this* she released her grasp on all she had lost and lifted up praise to God as she embraced the One who gives her breath.

Both of these stories inspire me. I'm not Lisa Beamer. And I'm not Gracia Burnham. I'm just a mom who has experienced a huge crisis with her son. But hearing the experiences of these women who have had great losses and traumatic transitions in their lives gives me hope that I, too, can make it in a world where everything doesn't turn out according to my expectations and dreams. Even if there is no happy ending to my family's story, other people who have experienced redemption in the midst of devastation help me find the strength to say, "I, too, will lay my Isaac down. I will refuse to try to explain away the pain in the world. I will not succumb to the temptation to quit sharing my story with others. I will embrace the One who loves me more than I love my Isaac."

HOPE FLOATS

The trial was once again scheduled to begin the last week of July 2001. It had been twenty-one months since Jason's arrest. Tension was high. Several family members had taken a week off work and had flown or driven to Florida at great expense to be in the courtroom to support our family. The Stretcher Bearers, this amazing group of supportive friends, sent us care packages filled with comfort foods, books, candles, tissues, bath products, and notes of encouragement, reminding us of their prayers as we entered into the week of the trial. We had flown Chelsea and Hannah to Michigan to stay with friends during this week of so much anxiety and unwanted publicity.

One couple who had encouraged us since the beginning of the crisis had rented a houseboat where some of the family members could have no-cost lodging and where we could cook some meals during the evenings in between long days in the courtroom. Our creative friends got together and decided to call the houseboat *Hope Floats,* the title of a movie starring Harry Connick Jr. and Sandra Bullock. Jason and April had seen the movie when they were falling in love, and that night, on their way out of the theater, J.P. picked up April and carried her out of the theater, reminiscent of the way Harry had come to the aid of Sandra in the film.

April had a framed picture of herself in Jason's arms with the *Hope Floats* movie marquee above their heads on that night, which now seemed so long ago. The picture was a visual reminder of a fairy-tale romance. How could a story that had such a perfect beginning have taken such a sad turn? Ginger, a friend who had flown in from San Diego to be supportive during the trial, had that picture blown up into a poster and laminated. It served as the captivating banner aboard the houseboat. HOPE FLOATS! I have heard television interviewer Dr. Freda Crews say, "Hope sets in motion the belief that things can change." How we needed that kind of hopeful momentum now!

Jury selection began on Monday morning. Several of our family members were in the courtroom. The attorney asked Gene and I not to be present that day. Day one progressed normally as several members of the jury were selected. About noon on day two, there was some murmuring at the desk of J.P.'s attorneys. Prosecutor Dorothy Sedgwick had referred to a specific page number in the documents of evidence, and it was soon disclosed that copies of approximately 250 pages of important papers had not been sent to Bill Barnett's office from the prosecutor's office. This was a major faux pas on the part of the prosecutor, and a huge matter of concern for Jason's attorney. The judge asked Bill Barnett to confer with his client and decide if they wanted to postpone the trial or continue.

With such a large body of paperwork that had not been analyzed, the decision was made to postpone the trial. The emotional impact of getting ready for our son's trial for first-degree murder and having the whole thing canceled after waiting for over a year and a half for resolution to this crisis felt devastating. There had been so much preparation, so much expense, and so much emotional energy expended on "the trial that wasn't," and I had no idea how much longer we would have to wait. Jason was once again put in leg irons, handcuffs, and a waist chain and ushered out of the courtroom to the holding room in the basement of the courthouse before being transported back to the jail in downtown Orlando.

There was part of me that thought, *Maybe God is up to something that we don't see on the surface. Carol, sit back and watch what God is going to do. There's a purpose in this delay. Be patient and don't lose hope.* Another part of me was desperate to know, *What is the point of this, God!?* I could feel anger boiling deep inside me and it didn't feel very righteous. My heart was screaming, "I absolutely can't take this! I am so frustrated, physically exhausted, emotionally spent, financially wrung out, and spiritually destitute." I wondered how much more relatives and friends would keep praying and supporting us when it seemed like we'd cried "Wolf!" so many times and the trial kept being postponed. My hope was far from floating — it was having a tough time treading water!

HOLDING ON *to* HOPE

Hope is another one of those remarkable words that can be both a verb and a noun. As a verb it means "to cherish a desire with anticipation, to desire with expectation of obtainment, to expect with confidence: trust."[3] As a noun, hope means "trust, reliance, a desire accompanied by expectation of or belief in fulfillment." It can also mean "someone or something on which hopes are centered."[4]

At different times during our unexpected journey, my emotional responses represented the embodiment of both the verb and the noun forms of hope. I hoped with anticipation that my son's defense would prevail: That he would be found temporarily insane at the time of his crime. J.P. believed that the man he killed posed a grave danger to Chelsea and Hannah. Even so, the action he took was against the laws of God and man, and therefore very wrong and grossly sinful. What would be a fair punishment for my son? We live in a society that, fortunately, does not allow people to take the law into their own hands. Some would say that if Jason was in his right mind at the time of the shooting, he deserves the death penalty. But I believe my son was mentally incapacitated at the time of the crime, and that he needs treatment and counseling in a controlled environment. A "not guilty by reason of temporary insanity" verdict certainly would not have meant instant freedom. At the judge's discretion, J.P probably would have been sent to a state mental hospital for an undetermined amount of time — at least ten years, if not much longer. But how I hoped that he would eventually be allowed to return to his family!

When hope is alive, there is always the chance that something that has gone awry will still have a positive outcome. We wait in anticipation of better news than we currently have. We hold on to hope in the waiting room of a hospital where, in another room, someone we love is undergoing life-threatening surgery. We watch the early pregnancy test with eager anticipation that the color we desire to see will appear, confirming the reality of a hoped-for baby. We give a spouse a second chance when we've been betrayed because we sincerely hope our marriage will last "'til death do us part." We go into a job interview in hope of being offered a position that will fit with our gifts and passions. We fervently hope our children will have a positive future. We hold on to the belief that even if what we see happening today is unbearable, ugly, unjust, and unfair, the probability of a brighter day is around the corner because God is the Great Redeemer.

KATIE'S STORY

When I first met Katie, she was a deeply committed Christian and successful businesswoman. Against all odds, she clung to the only hope she had — a reliance, trust, and confidence in a God who could bring healing to her unthinkable circumstances. Here is her story in her own words:

> The call came from the child welfare agency. They asked me to come to their office about a matter concerning my daughter Lindsey. With keys in hand, I was ready to take my younger daughter, Susan, to a

dental appointment and explained that it would be better if my husband could meet with them instead of me. "No," came the reply, "we'd rather *you* come."

"Well, what does this involve?" I asked.

"We can't talk to you about it over the phone, but if you come down here, we'll explain everything," the gentle voice responded.

"Should I call my husband? Does he need to be there too?"

"No, we don't want to involve him at this time."

I suddenly understood the urgency of this call, and as I hung up the phone, the reality of what was possible began to sink in. I called my boss, a fellow Christian who had seen her own share of family heartache. I told her of the conversation and she prayed with me. I could sense that she suspected what I did.

The next few hours were surreal — a confrontation with the police, special detectives, and child advocacy personnel who sat me down in a room and tried to tell me as kindly as possible that my child had accused her father of sexually molesting her. My thoughts ran the gamut: *It can't be true. She's got to be lying*, to *That filthy jerk! What is WRONG with him?* I could not conceive of the fact that the man I knew so well, the man I slept beside for over twenty years, the husband who had served the Lord in a wide variety of ministry roles, could possibly be capable of such a wicked and disgusting thing. But he was.

The next few months were a blur — going through the court proceedings, understanding my husband's mental health condition, analyzing our marriage, our parenting, our pain, and our own self-deception. In the state where we reside, my husband received ninety days of jail time at a halfway house and five years of probation. His crime was a felony offense, and his sentence included a sexual offender treatment program, regular polygraph tests, and very tight restrictions.

I was angry and hurt, and I had lost all trust in Craig — as a husband, as a father, and as a Christian. My husband had turned my world upside-down. I desperately tried to cope with my horrific emotions and the needs of my two hurting daughters. *How could Craig have crossed that line? How could he have been so selfish? How could he have pretended to be so spiritual while involved in such abhorrent behavior? How could his values be so different from mine?*

People wondered if I would leave my husband. In some ways, it might have been easier than the path we chose. But I will tell you about our journey back from the brink, the story of a marriage nearly destroyed, but one that is still being healed today. Craig and I started to find answers and hope, together.

In deep anguish for the pain he caused his family, his church, and himself, my husband repented of his sin. He immediately informed our pastor and made himself accountable to him. Craig contacted a marriage counselor for help and then asked me to join him. Our church home group held a prayer meeting, inviting the leadership to come and talk and pray with us. We were able to honestly share where we were in our marriage and in the legal process. This small group has now turned into a prayer support team of more than thirty people. We e-mail this group regularly with our prayer needs, our concerns, our victories, and our defeats.

Craig's last day at home was the morning my daughter told her school counselor what had happened. He was not allowed back in our home. He has lived with friends who had no children at home, and he was cut off from attending church or going to any public places where children might congregate. Our meeting places were limited, and the two of us usually met in the room he rented from our friends.

We found out about a highly effective fourteen-week marriage program, and we met together twice a week to complete the course. Our Christian counselor also helped us to find the road to recovery. As we worked individually and together week after week, we found the trust slowly rebuilding, the masks coming off, and the truth coming out. To our surprise, as time went on, we found ourselves falling in love with each other all over again. We continued with our Christian counselor, read a variety of helpful Christian books, studied Proverbs together, and followed all of the legally imposed restrictions and rehabilitation guidelines.

Because his treatment program doesn't allow Craig to attend church, we have met for over three years on Sunday mornings at our local hospital chapel to hold our own "small group." We've worked slowly through four intensive Bible studies, doing the work at home, and coming together to discuss it in the chapel. We have learned much about each other and about God. Craig has learned how to cherish me, and I have learned how to respect him again. The chapel has become a sanctuary for us and a very special house of worship.

Over many months we have progressed from supervised meetings with our youngest daughter, to being allowed to include our oldest daughter, to meeting together in public places for approved amounts of time, to family therapy sessions. Lindsey, by God's grace and through the influence of a youth pastor who had also been abused as a child, found it in her heart to forgive her father after much travail in prayer.

I have my husband back, and after an excruciatingly difficult experience, I also have two beautiful daughters back. God has restored appropriate love in our family and made it better than it was before. It has been a complicated journey, but last Christmas Craig was allowed in our home for the first time in over four years. Our story is one of love, redemption, and reconciliation. I have learned the truth of the proverb: "Hope deferred makes the heart sick, but when dreams come true, there is life and joy."[5]

My friend Donna's story is very different, but as I thought about it during our months of excruciating loss and limbo, I was buoyed by the reminder that even when all hope is extinguished, God does not forsake His children — even when they forsake Him. Donna had to lay her expectations about marriage, parenting, ministry, and "the perfect Christian life" on the altar. Her story does not end like Abraham's, but she found her hope in the God of redemption, the same God Abraham knew.

I didn't know that it was God who was asking me to lay my Isaac down when I heard my former husband say the words that changed my life forever. "Donna, I don't know if I love you. I don't know if I've ever loved you. I think I want a divorce."

As I began the horrific legal, emotional, and spiritual journey of dissolving a twenty-year marriage and starting a new life, I felt more like an "Isaac" than someone who was being called by God to new levels of faith. Unlike Abraham, my surrender was not voluntary. I didn't courageously climb up the mountain expecting God to provide. Instead, it seemed like I was the victim as I watched God rip away all that I felt was important in my life. In one fell swoop I lost my family, my community, my security, my ministry, and my ability to trust God to take care of me.

One of my first prayers as a Christian was for my marriage. I knew we were in serious trouble. My husband had a volatile temper, was extremely controlling, and frequently violent. I was afraid of him. I suspected infidelity. I now understand that I didn't have a clue about his secret life. I later discovered that he was not only having affairs, but was also a voyeur. His inhibitions were deadened by substance abuse, and he spent night after night wandering through neighborhoods peering into other people's bedroom windows. Sometimes he broke into homes. My tentative inquiries as to his whereabouts were met with rage so extreme that I quickly learned not to ask. My affectionate feelings for him were all but dead.

One child later, and on the verge of divorce, I met Jesus. The Holy Spirit moved in and gave me what I did not have without Him. Love. Joy. Peace. Patience. Kindness. Goodness. Faithfulness. Gentleness. Self-control. God gave me hope. He helped me to see Roy through the blood of Christ and forgive. He gave me wisdom. He

helped me to not only endure but to grow in my difficult circumstances. When Roy met Jesus too, I thought our troubles were over.
For a while, it seemed that they were. Roy began to grow spiritually.
Doors began to open in ministry and, encouraged by my husband,
I began to travel and speak at retreats and conferences. Our second
child was born. Life was wonderful. At least I thought so. What I
didn't know was that when I was gone, Roy was once again engaging
in his pre-Christian behaviors.

He was arrested in the bedroom of an undercover policeman. I
sat by his side in the courtroom and prayed as he pled "no contest"
to the charges. The judge let him go with a stern warning. It was a
slap on the wrist by a legal system that didn't seem to understand the
nature of his problem.

The policeman was a member of our local Christian community
and recognized my name. Soon my pastor was informed. I again sat
by my husband's side in the pastor's office and prayed and watched
a godly man with an enormous heart but no understanding of the
nature of the problem try to intervene. I begged God to help us, to
rescue my husband, to throw us a lifeline. Rescue never came. Instead,
embarrassed, my husband stopped attending church. His secret
behaviors became less and less secret and began to take over our lives.

I began to seek help for myself by attending Al-Anon meetings.
To the degree that my behavior grew less codependent, his grew
increasingly hostile. Just before the end of our marriage he said, "I am
at war with God."

I responded. "How sad. You'll lose."

After the divorce, life as I knew it ended. My divorce attorney
knew I couldn't afford to fight; many important details fell through
the cracks. I received no alimony after twenty years of marriage. Roy
quit his job, so for many months I didn't receive child support. We
had to sell our home to pay our debt. We divided the rest. All the
while I prayed. I begged God to rescue us, to provide for me and for

my children. I watched the thicket, but no ram was provided. I held on to hope.

I had not been employed in the secular arena for most of my adult life. Knowing my honorariums would not be sufficient to cover our expenses, I looked for work. I took a job as a receptionist that paid very little, but promised advancement. I trusted God to provide.

I held on to hope when my two children and I squeezed into a two-bedroom apartment in a bad neighborhood in a new community, because it was all I could afford. My daughter and I shared a bed. We lived off the home sale proceeds and my minimum wage job. I ate oatmeal for nearly a year because it was all I could afford.

I held on to hope when simply surviving took all of my effort. In the divorce, I was "awarded" a car badly in need of maintenance and worth much less than what was owed. Early one winter morning as I was driving to work, it gasped its last breath. This ending came after months and months of "Band-aid" repairs to escalating problems. The death of the car was very dramatic, with loud grinding metal against metal and black smoke billowing from under the hood. I abandoned the vehicle on the side of the road and walked several miles home in the cold in high-heeled shoes and a light coat, crying all the way. Unable to afford further repairs and unwilling to make payments on a car I could not drive, I called the lending company and told them where they could pick up the vehicle.

I held on to hope for restoration of my ministry, even as I gave away my library and discarded the contents of my filing cabinet, because there was no room for them in my little apartment. In the years that followed, I struggled with jealousy as I watched others step into ministry positions that were once mine. I struggled with resentment when I witnessed my friends' delight in what God was doing in their lives and their ministries. I struggled with self-pity as I drove my one-hour commute to a low-paying job that was in no way an expression of my God-given gifts and abilities. I struggled, but I held on to hope.

I also held on to hope for my family when my teenage children began to take full advantage of a mother who worked long hours and was too exhausted and overwhelmed to be an effective parent alone. During those terrible years I lived through all of my "worst-case" parent scenarios. In alphabetical order, here is a partial listing: Delinquency. Hostility. Promiscuity. Rebellion. Substance abuse.

I began to lose hope when, with no health insurance, I discovered a pronounced lump in my lower abdomen. I decided not to have it examined. I could not afford a doctor's office visit, much less surgery or time off for recovery. Whether it was cancer or not ceased to be an issue. In fact, death seemed to be a much-welcomed escape from the pain of living. Several years later, when I was finally able to secure health insurance, the lump was diagnosed to be a large ovarian tumor. At that time it required a total hysterectomy.

The end of hope came when my daughter decided she did not want to live with me anymore because I had rules to obey. She wanted to go and live with her father, who was living in a friend's basement and was never at home. A sight that is forever engraved on my mind's eye is my precious fourteen-year-old daughter sitting stubbornly on the stoop of our apartment waiting for her dad to come and pick her up. All of her belongings were shoved into two garbage bags beside her. I left her there and drove to work. I didn't hear from her or see her for over three months. During the time she lived with her dad, she seldom saw him. Her basic needs of food and supervision were not met. It was a real descent into darkness for her as she did whatever she pleased with her life. For me, it was the end of faith.

In all of this, well-meaning friends promised, "God will provide." I was painfully aware that Christians throughout the centuries had waited for God to provide — and at times it seems He didn't. Those devoted believers facing lions in Caesar's arena prayed for a "Daniel" experience that never came. Those steadfast saints on the *Titanic* prayed to be given the gift of water-walking, as had been given Peter (or, at the very least, for a lifeboat). They took their last breaths in the icy water hoping God would provide. I suddenly understood that God does not always provide a rescue. I lost hope and I walked away from the God I thought had failed me. For seven years I lived as if He did not exist.

"In the fullness of time" God, in His grace, called me back. He reminded me of His love for me, of His goodness even when I couldn't see it. A passage I had memorized from the Psalms years before came back to me: "*I would have despaired* unless I had believed that I would see the goodness of the LORD in the land of the living. Wait for the LORD; be strong, and let your heart take courage; yes, wait for the LORD."[6]

In the Song of Songs, Shulamite rejected her lover and then regretted her decision. She began to long for him. She began to look for him. "I looked for the one my heart loves," she says, "I looked for him but did not find him." The search took her many places. Then, suddenly, there he was! She said, "When I found the one my heart loves, I held him and would not let him go." Her story became my story as I was reconciled to the Lover of my soul.

I went on to gain a degree of success in the secular arena. I also remarried. When I sensed God calling me back to full-time Christian service, I was terrified. I didn't know if other Christians would receive me. After all, mine was not a sweet "victory" story! But God's Spirit whispered, "I'm not asking you to trust Me. I am teaching you (present tense, continuing action) to trust Me. Just take the next step." One step led to another, and another, which led to today. I am currently on the staff of a large church as the director of women's ministries and director of small group leadership development. I'm surprised and delighted to find myself here.

It would be nice to end this by saying "and they all lived happily ever after." That would not be true. There are areas where I still wait to see "the goodness of the Lord in the land of the living," as I watch the lives of my children, and now my grandchildren. But now I wait in hope, in strength, and in courage, because I know my Redeemer lives, and His heart toward me is good.

THE POWER *of* HOPE

Gabriel Marcel defines hope as "a memory of the future."[7] This kind of hope means that we are as convinced about what is going to happen (the future we are positively envisioning) as we are about the certainty of what has already taken place (the past).

Hope becomes unsinkable when we realize our hope is not in having spouses or friends who will never disappoint us, or in enjoying financial security, or in achieving a certain level of success, or in having perfect health, or in watching children turn out exactly as we had anticipated. Hope remains constant when we get to know the Source of all hope.

Perhaps the psalmist said it best:

I wait quietly before God, for my hope is in him. He alone is my rock and my salvation, my fortress where I will not be shaken. My salvation and my honor come from God alone. He is my refuge, a rock where no enemy can reach me.[8]

Hope's power is that we have the energy and desire to go on living because we believe something better is coming. That's the bottom line for the Christian: *Something more is coming.* There is more to this world than meets the eye. No matter what happens to you or your family, no matter what disappointments you encounter, no matter what diagnosis the doctor gives you, even if the end result is physical death, there is still *something more.*

But we're not home yet. So my encouragement for today is that if I put my hope in the Lord, there are great benefits. Isaiah once said, "Those who hope in the LORD will renew their strength. They will soar on wings like eagles; they will run and not grow weary, they will walk and not be faint."[9]

Looking back on Abraham's total commitment to living out God's purpose for his life, I realize that understanding the covenant God made with him earlier gave Abraham hope, confidence, focus, and the ability to trust God when he faced hopeless situations and challenges — like being asked to sacrifice Isaac on the altar.

> Against all hope, Abraham in hope believed and so became the father of many nations, just as it had been said to him, "So shall your offspring be." Without weakening in his faith, he faced the fact that his body was as good as dead — since he was about a hundred years old — and that Sarah's womb was also dead. Yet he did not waver through unbelief regarding the promise of God, but was strengthened in his faith and gave glory to God, being fully persuaded that God had power to do what he had promised. This is why "it was credited to him as righteousness."[10]

Henry Blackaby has written an entire book on Abraham entitled, *Created to Be God's Friend: How God Shapes Those He Loves.* Blackaby asks,

> Have you ever felt the magnitude of God's encounter with you? Have you so sensed His eternal purpose through you that you have radically and thoroughly released your will to His will, and your heart to His Heart? Have you been progressively experiencing God's shaping your character to match His assignment in your life? . . . Every Christian is . . . called by God to be on a mission with Him in His world.[11]

Even reading the questions above fills me with hope. I know that in the midst of my personal circumstances, which at times have felt hopeless and pointless, God is intimately involved in shaping the core of me because He loves me. I also know that I have an eternal purpose, and I want to radically and thoroughly release my will to His will — for myself, for my son, for my family. I believe that even in a courtroom in Orlando, Florida, where a decision impacting the rest of my son's life will be determined, every person in my family is on a mission of great importance to God simply because they are part of *His* family and *His* plan.

As Gene and I agonized for our son and as all of us continued to wait for the trial, which was again postponed for another interminable five months, a long-anticipated call came from our attorney. Bill Barnett's words brought renewed hope to parents who were in great pain. "I've called to tell you that Dorothy Sedgwick (the prosecutor) has informed our office that she will not seek the death penalty in the case against Jason." While he still faced the potential of life in prison without the possibility of parole, we knew that at least one of our hopes had been fulfilled.

God's Power in *Your* Circumstances

Hope floats because it has an anchor. "We have this hope as an anchor for the soul, firm and secure."[12] Gregory Floyd said it well: "Hope is symbolized in Christian iconography by an anchor. And what does an anchor do? It keeps the ship on course when wind and waves rage against it. But the anchor of hope is sunk in heaven, not on earth."[13]

The Bible is filled with references to hope — where it comes from, the way we can demonstrate it, and the process that produces it.

- We obtain hope through promises in God's Word. (Romans 15:4)
- We have hope because of the victorious resurrection of Christ.
  (1 Peter 1:3)
- Our happiness comes through hope in God. (Psalm 146:5)
- Our suffering produces hope, if we allow suffering to strengthen our character. (Romans 5:2-4)
- Hope is never disappointing. (Romans 5:5)

All these truths can buoy us when we feel we are sinking into a sea of despair.

1. In what specific area or circumstance in your life today are you holding on to hope? What exactly have you been hoping for? Has anything you've read in this chapter altered your position or perspective in any way? If so, write down what has challenged or encouraged you and ask God to reveal more to you in the days ahead.

2. Is there an area or circumstance in your life about which you have lost hope? If so, why? Write out Psalm 62:5-7 on an index card, and place it where you can read it often. Memorize it and then intentionally meditate on it every day for at least one week. At the end of that week, notice if anything about your attitude or position has changed.

3. Think back on your life and ask God to bring to mind times when He has brought some kind of victory out of calamity. Consider designating a small notebook or journal in which you will record past and future "evidence" of "God's great salvage operation of redemption." How could such a record buoy your hope?

4. On page 94 I wrote: "The 'even in this' category of suffering makes the small stuff truly small, because what we have to deal with puts the rest of life into perspective." How have you experienced this to be true in the past or present? Consider the "stuff" you are currently dealing with. Is some of it "smaller" than you have been making it?

5. During my Isaac experience I have drawn comfort and hope from the tragic but redemptive stories of people like Lisa Beamer and Gracia Burnham. Who do you know, personally or by reputation, whose experience of redemption in the midst of devastation demonstrates the power of hope? Write this person a note of thanks for their role as a hope-giver and, if possible, send it to them.

6. Do you agree with Henry Blackaby's bold statement: "Every Christian is called by God to be on a mission with Him in His world"? How would you describe the mission you believe you are on at this time in your life?

chapter six

BUT *W*HERE IS THE LAMB?

The Power *of* Faith

*The kind of faith God values seems to develop best when everything
fuzzes over, when God stays silent, when the fog rolls in.*
—PHILIP YANCEY

TWO MONTHS BEFORE OUR SON'S TRIAL WAS TO BEGIN IN
December, the United States was reeling from the events of September 11,
2001. A new inmate had recently been moved into J.P.'s cellblock. Andre (not
his real name) had been a member of the French Foreign Legion, and he spoke
five languages, including Arabic and Farsi. These two young men bonded, and
they spent many hours together studying Scripture and discussing their military
backgrounds.

Before long Jason realized that Andre had intimate knowledge regarding
terrorist cells in the United States and Canada, but with English as his second
language, Andre couldn't clearly communicate what he knew, and he didn't
know who to trust. Jason talked at length to Andre about the need to contact
U.S. officials to inform them of this timely and sensitive information. Andre
had a public defender he didn't trust, but he gave Jason permission to make
contact with governmental agencies. Within a couple of days, J.P. got word to
the Federal Bureau of Investigation, and Andre was taken out of confinement
for a polygraph test, which he passed.

For the next few weeks there was a blur of activity as officials scheduled numerous interviews with Andre to try to get to the bottom of the knowledge he had that might be valuable to U.S. intelligence. Andre gave the agents enough verifiable information to prove that he had strong credibility, but he withheld additional sensitive information, hoping for a plea bargain arrangement for himself and for Jason.

Government officials believed the information Andre had was important enough to national security that they were willing to continue dialoguing with him about what he knew and what plea bargain options might be possible. With less than a week to go before the start of Jason's trial, we were told that it had once again been continued. A seventh postponement was devastating; however, once we were told that the delay was due to national security issues, our hope soared and our faith increased. *Could this be the reason for the earlier postponement of the trial? Was God orchestrating this delay so that J.P's timely connection with Andre could result in an out-of-court resolution instead of a trial?*

The next few months were tense. All Americans were wondering when and where there would be another terrorist attack. However, as month followed month, there was less fear and less urgency; the importance of Andre's information to governmental authorities didn't seem as valuable. Our great hopes were dissipating, and walking by faith was again a daunting task.

WALKING *by* FAITH

Jim Cymbala aptly describes faith:

> What is faith? It is total dependence on God that becomes supernatural in its working. People with faith develop a second kind of sight. They see more than just the circumstances; they see God right beside them. Can they prove it? No. But by faith they know he's there. . . . Faith alone is the trigger that releases driving power.[1]

I believe Cymbala's definition of faith from the bottom of my feet to the top of my head. When God walks beside us, the faith journey is an adventure like none other. It's a road with surprising twists and turns, sometimes with deep ruts and uneven surfaces, but it's always filled with enough road markers to get us to the next juncture. I needed that kind of faith now more than ever.

Looking back, I realized a significant way in which God prepared me for the months leading up to the trial. I didn't know what lay ahead of us and how much I needed heart preparation to endure the coming events, but I had two friends with a sweet sense of urgency about the role God wanted them to play in this waiting-room experience.

Karen Beck and Bette Jo Nienhuis had been friends for many years, but moves due to career and ministry opportunities had transitioned us to cities that were more than four hours from each other. Both of these women sent multiple notes of encouragement during the long months of our ordeal, but toward the end of the summer of 2001 they insisted on seeing me in person. Graciously, they asked if I would come for an overnight at Karen's vacation home on a lake near Angola, Indiana.

After arriving in the late afternoon with my overnight bag in hand, I realized the enormous amount of preparation these friends had put into our getaway. They greeted me warmly and led me to one of the guest rooms where they gave me leisurely time to unpack. When I emerged, the dinner table was set exquisitely, and I realized they had painstakingly developed a menu for our retreat that included many homemade specialties. They also had bread and bagels from a favorite bakery, gourmet dips and sauces, and freshly brewed coffee and tea. We enjoyed a rare evening of long, uninterrupted conversation, authentic revelations about our hopes and fears for our family members, and our growing and stretching experiences with God and faith issues. My time with them was a relaxing and deeply nurturing "pause" in the middle of much stress.

The next morning we adopted an unhurried stay-in-your-robe-as-long-as-you-want mode and had coffee on the deck overlooking the lake. I was once again treated as a special guest who was being served with loving care and deep compassion. In the early hours of the afternoon we curled up on big overstuffed sofas in the informal great room. Karen and Bette Jo then did something I had never before observed or experienced. They made me their "audience of one" and ministered to me. They read Scriptures on faith and hope; they prayed over me, personally naming each of my family members who were impacted by our crisis. They prayed for J.P.'s attorney, for the prosecutor, for the judge, and for God to superintend every aspect of the jury selection.

The last thing they did moved me to tears, and thoughts of it now, more than two-and-a-half years later, linger like a sweet fragrance. They got out old hymnbooks and sang to me of God's faithfulness. Neither of them is a trained musician, but they were teaching me by example the power of faith, expressed in worship and praise, in a dark hour. They sang in unison, "Great is Thy faithfulness, O God, my Father. There is no shadow of turning with Thee. Thou changest not, Thy compassions they fail not. As Thou hast been, Thou forever wilt be."[2] As their duet continued, Karen and Bette Jo maintained tender eye contact with me. By the time they got to the chorus, I tried to join them, but my voice started cracking as I saw the tears flowing down the cheeks of my friends. We spent the next hour moving from hymn to hymn — "A Mighty Fortress Is Our God," "Be Thou My Vision," "O God Our Help in Ages Past, Our Hope for Years to Come," and "Amazing Grace." The music from my earliest years in church, mingled with tears and the outpouring of love and compassion from these creative and remarkable friends, was a powerful, grace-filled road marker on my faith journey. Little did I know how much I would lean back into that experience of love and worship during the next several months of twists and turns, ruts and valleys.

By this time our family had hundreds of e-mail prayer warriors, and I could sense the driving power of all of those intercessors as we entered the new year. I could not actually see Him, but I knew God was walking beside us as we continued to get closer to the legal process that would determine the rest of our son's life. I had absolute faith that God could do *anything*—and that He would be glorified in the process, no matter what the outcome of the trial.

While trying to concentrate on choosing faith over worry, I read this brief story recorded by Max Lucado:

An example of faith was found on the wall of a concentration camp. On it a prisoner had carved the words:

I believe in the sun, even though it doesn't shine,

I believe in love, even when it isn't shown,

I believe in God, even when he doesn't speak.

I try to imagine the person who etched those words. I try to envision his skeletal hand gripping the broken glass or stone that cut into the wall. I try to imagine his eyes squinting through the darkness as he carved each letter. What hand could have cut such a conviction? What eyes could have seen good in such horror?

There is only one answer: Eyes that chose to see the unseen.[3]

That story bothered me because even though the prisoner obviously had great faith, there wasn't a happy ending. My God was a rescuing God, a very present help in the time of trouble, a God of miracles and second chances, a God who heard and answered prayer, a God of mercy and grace. I *thought* I had mountain-moving faith. The Bible was filled with examples of that kind of faith, and I had memorized the details of those faith-stories. Baby Moses' life was spared in the bulrushes. Israel walked through the Red Sea on dry ground. The Israelites marched around the walls of Jericho for seven days and the walls fell flat. Rahab welcomed the spies and escaped the destruction that came to those who refused to trust God. Daniel was protected in the lion's den and in the fiery furnace. Peter was released from prison while there was a prayer meeting taking place on his behalf. Paul and Silas were set free by a violent earthquake, and they turned their release into a ministry opportunity.

Thinking of all these miraculous rescues and divine interventions I couldn't help but wonder, *What might God do for my son if we had enough faith to believe He could do the impossible?* If the resolution was not favorable, would it be our fault for not having "enough" faith? There had been so many postponements, followed by multiple encouragements during the months prior to the trial. The vast army of people who were praying for the case was increasing daily. Could all of this be the making of a miracle?

But unlike Daniel, Peter, Paul, or Silas, our son was not incarcerated under false accusations. His finger pulled the trigger and a man died. As the next few months passed, there were many days when fear won over faith in my heart.

One of those days was when another letter arrived, on official government stationery, informing us that Jason's trial had been rescheduled for April 15, 2002. As I held the sterile, impersonal letter in my hand, I realized that everything that paper represented would ultimately determine the rest of my son's life. A cold shiver crawled up my body, and waves of doubt and fear flooded my mind. Thoughts flowed uncontrollably: *In over two years the prosecutor has not approached J.P.'s attorney with a plea bargain offer. She's had over twenty years of experience before judges and juries. Why did we get this woman as our prosecutor? Most other attorneys would have settled this case out of court. I am so afraid. Fear is clouding my ability to think calmly or rationally. When J.P. calls home, I try to give him hope; but my real feelings are so intensely terrorizing that I'm afraid to speak of them out loud because I don't want to drag him or others down with me.*

I placed the letter on Gene's desk and walked into another room. I wanted to be physically removed from the paperwork that represented the magnitude and intensity of my fears. The familiar nausea that often accompanied my darkest moments overwhelmed me. I felt sick to the core of my soul.

Another man felt this excruciating and disorienting soul sickness right before he was called to step out in faith in a very different way. Not all of life's worst terrors press in from outside. Sometimes the "Isaac" God asks us to lay down is rooted deep within. Here is Vince's story, in his own words.

A DIFFERENT TEST *of* FAITH

It was 4:30 P.M., our usual time to "check in."

"Hi, Vince." Her voice on the phone was flat. Normally it was vital and warm; I could always "hear" her beautiful smile. She had become such a delightful presence in my life over the past several months — even though our time to connect was excruciatingly limited.

"Hi, Beautiful," I said, hoping to melt the coldness I heard in her voice. We chitchatted for a minute or so, while I felt an icy dread creep up my spine. Suddenly she said it. "It's really hard to talk about 'us.'" I braced myself. "But I can't meet you for dinner. I just know I can't do this anymore."

I was silent. A lead ball — my heart — fell with a sickening thud from my chest to my stomach.

"I'm *so* sorry," she said.

"I understand," I replied calmly. *No, no, no, no!*

"Vince . . ." Her voice quivered. My hopes soared.

"Meagan, I . . ."

"Bye," she said. The line went dead.

Just like that. It was over.

"It" had been "no big deal." *At least not in any sane person's mind,* I spit at myself contemptuously. Meagan and I had "just" been friends. I knew that was all we could ever be. My head knew it, anyway. My heart was a different territory entirely. I could hear a raw, icy whistling through the hole that had just been knifed through my chest.

I had met Meagan and her husband, Joe, at a dinner party at a mutual friend's house. I liked them both instantly. They were warm, winsome, open-hearted people. They seemed like the perfect couple. And yet I could sense a quiet sadness in Meagan. When we started meeting "innocently" over a rushed dinner or cup of coffee, I learned that her "perfect" marriage was indeed good in many ways, but very lonely in others. Joe was devoted to her — and she to him — but he couldn't express his love in the tender ways she craved. The ways we were discovering I could express it. The ways she expressed it to me.

I lost myself in the deep pools of this gentle woman's robin's-egg-blue eyes. She had a way of looking at me with a tenderness that touched me so deeply, my heart was irrevocably gone. For the first time in my thirty-nine years, I was experiencing what it was like to be *seen* — seen *through*, it seemed. *What was this?* No one had ever looked at me with such kindness, such *intensity*. It wasn't lust. At first I couldn't even categorize it as romantic. All I knew was that my heart was being caressed so intimately that I would never be able to look at this woman casually again.

And that was a big problem. Because I knew that Meagan could never give me any of the "more" I suddenly craved to the core of my soul. And I did want so much more. So did Meagan. We knew the relationship was on a fast track to a full-blown affair. I had ridden those rails before. I didn't want to be part of another train wreck. I knew God didn't want me to be. Neither of us would ever be able to live with ourselves if she left Joe for me. At least she had concluded that she wouldn't be able to.

And so she said goodbye . . . before I could. I wasn't ready. I probably never would have been ready. After all, I had made it my lifetime habit to subsist on the "leftovers" from other people's hearts.

I swear I remember feeling a "hole in my soul" before I could even talk. As an infant I had been emotionally abandoned by both my parents when their marriage hit the skids right before I was born. I spent my entire childhood trying to be good enough, cute enough, big enough, funny enough, *something* enough to get my frazzled, disengaged single mother to adore me. Instead, she practically abhorred me. I reminded her of my "no-good father." I could never win her heart. So I ran around like a puppy nipping at her heels, begging for a crumb of goodwill to drop accidentally from her hand. Once in a while it did, and I would hoard it like it was a huge wedge of rich chocolate cake. I would nibble on any morsel of kindness for days. *This is better than nothing,* I vividly remember thinking as a little boy. *I'm lucky to get this much.*

By the time I was a young man I almost prided myself on needing virtually nothing in my relationships. I was "the rock," "the shoulder to lean on," "the bridge over troubled waters" to a seemingly endless parade of people who "needed" me. My role kept me very busy. Very "useful," I thought, even strong. After all, no one knew that the "rock" was mostly hollow. No one knew that at the core of "Steady Eddie" was a toxic waste dump of shame that kept me feeling perpetually unlovable, unknowable, untouchable. I was never really "happy" being used instead of loved, *but it was better than nothing.* And it was all

I was going to get in this world; that much I knew. *Count your blessings*, I always told myself. For a guy whose own mother didn't love him, I wasn't doing so bad.

But now . . . at almost forty . . . I was doing *bad*. In fact, after Meagan hung up I didn't know how I was going to continue breathing. I didn't want to. Somehow Meagan had managed to touch "the untouchable." Her tenderness had been like a soothing balm to my leprous soul. Her withdrawal, which my head "understood" completely, felt like the end of me. *Why?* It wasn't like I hadn't been "left" before. I was familiar with rejection. Surely I could pull myself up by my bootstraps as I always had and get back to the business of being useful. I didn't need anything. I couldn't want anything. "Longing" was for sissies. It didn't have a place in my carefully crafted self-sufficient script.

But after putting the phone back in its cradle, I found myself, "the rock," crumbled on the floor of my home office. A moment before I had been a grown man; now I was a squalling, abandoned baby. I couldn't believe the sounds that were coming out of me. Meagan's "bye" hit me like lava flowing across a glacier. I was choking on a lifetime's backwash of frozen tears.

I didn't think I could ever get up off the floor. I didn't want to. My limbs felt as paralyzed as my heart. Dead. Impotent. Why, God . . . why? Why did You let me meet that sweet-hearted angel if You knew this was going to be the result? Why didn't You stop me from letting her warmth into my heart when You had no future planned for "us"? What do You expect me to do from here? What good is a rock that is now a puddle? I can't even move. I can't even breathe. I don't want to.

As the late afternoon sun faded I continued to lie there, spent and undone. Darkness settled in. I wished I could fade into it and never see daylight again. I knew I would never see Meagan's blue eyes again. Worst of all, I knew I could never believe my own best line again. Better than nothing . . . Better than nothing . . . No, I could never again be satisfied with crumbs and leftovers. Meagan had awakened a hunger in me that I had spent my whole life trying not to feel. And now she was irrevocably gone. I had never felt so alone.

"Do you want to get well?"

What? I could swear I heard a voice, gentle in the darkness.

"Do you want to get well?"

Suddenly I recognized the question. Jesus had asked it of a paralyzed man in the gospel of John.[4] I had always thought it a very odd question. The guy had been lying in the same spot for *thirty-eight years*, for heaven's sake — wishing only that he could get to the healing pool just beyond his reach. Jesus' question had always sounded almost like a taunt to me.

"Do You think I'm *enjoying* lying here on the floor?" I shouted into the darkness. "Do You think I've *enjoyed* being a yipping dog all my life, begging for crumbs from other people's tables? How dare You ask me what I want anyway? You don't care what I want. You have never had any intention of giving me what I want. I've tried to be Your man anyway. I've tried to give, to love, to 'be there' for everyone. I'm sick of it! I'm sick of this life. I'M SICK! Why are You asking me such a stupid question? *Of course* I want to get well!"

"Get up, then."

"*What?*"

"Start walking."

"Walking toward what?! You've just called my number again. 'Hey everybody, here's Vince, the unlovable. Let's give him a hand while he gets up on all fours and yips his way through some more years of begging for crumbs.' No thanks! I'll stay right where I am. Find someone else to play this role in Your drama."

My ruthless sarcasm didn't seem to faze this evening Visitor. "This is not My drama, My son. It is yours."

His tone was so firm, yet kind. I was stumped for a cutting comeback.

"I never assigned this role to you," He continued. "Do you want to get well?"

There's that stupid question again, I thought.

"What do You want from me?!" I tried to feel angry, but my voice came out as a sob tinged with hope. *Could He really be offering me a different life after all these years?*

"I want you to dump your paralyzing, undeserved shame and walk toward Me. The healing pool is right here. Follow the sound of My voice."

The sound was a distant melody. My soul craned to hear its beauty more clearly. "I want to," I whispered. "I want to get well. I want to follow You."

"Come, then. Leave your tattered rags of shame and come to Me. In My eyes you are so much more than 'enough.' Come, look at Me."

He seemed as close as my breath now. Maybe I could reach Him if I just . . . looked up.

His eyes were deep pools of robin's-egg blue.

Six months have passed since that encounter with a love that will not let me go. I eventually did get up off the floor, but I don't know where I am going. I hear no clear Voice of direction now, no promises of a human relationship that will once again touch my now broken-open heart. Some days I crave the darkness; hiding my heart is familiar and feels safer than walking free of the shame that hisses, "Who do you think you are? Someone worth *lov*i*ng*?" Could I really become some*one*, not just some*thing* dumped on this planet to be a service provider? Most days I still doubt it. And I'm terrified to be vulnerable to another person who could "get to me" like Meagan did. Surely it would only end badly, as always. And yet I cannot forget: "Leave your tattered rags," the tender invitation to live a different script than I learned from my mother.

"Now faith is confidence in what we hope for and assurance about what we do not see,"[5] the book of Hebrews tells us. The man who had not had the use of his limbs for thirty-eight years must have had that blind faith, or else how could he have responded to Jesus' nonsensical command to "Get up! Pick up your mat and walk!"[6] The guy knew he couldn't do that! And yet something moved his frozen body. He was healed on the spot and walked away, free. Obviously it was a miracle . . . and I know I need a miracle in order to be healed from a lifetime of living a script God apparently never intended. But something about the paralyzed man's story shouts to me that the miracle that day took place in his heart before it moved to his limbs. He chose to *believe,* even in his unbelief, in the possibility of what he hadn't experienced in nearly four decades — perhaps never.

I wonder what role that man went on to play in God's grand story. I wonder what new script God has for me. I have laid down my cynicism on the altar, along with my rags of shame. I feel buck naked. But as He washes away the grime from my soul with His healing water, I feel bathed in a love that will never say, "Bye." He has offered me a permanent seat at His banquet table, where there is plenty of rich fare for everyone. When I feel the old inclination to crawl under the table and yip for crumbs, He firmly asks me again, "Do you want to get well?" I no longer think it's a stupid or taunting question. I hear the tender invitation to focus my eyes on His once again, and to lose myself in His blue pools of grace.

I miss Meagan. Terribly. Maybe I always will. But I can see her now as the sweet-hearted angel she truly was. She "left" me to the true Lover of my soul. His name is Jesus. And every day at 4:30 I stop whatever I'm doing to "check in" with Him. He hasn't stood me up once. He never hangs up when I'm in the middle of a sentence.

I am no longer a "rock." I'm not sure what I am yet. But I have found a Rock that is higher than I.[7] And I am beginning to believe that He and I, together, are "enough."

Vince may never know the fulfillment of one of his heart's deepest longings: a relationship with a human, someone who is free to lavish him with all the love he deserves. But he is on his feet anyway, walking toward the promise of a shame-free life. He is choosing to lay down his self-contempt and cynicism and replace it with faith in an ancient promise that underlies all others: "The eternal God is your refuge, and underneath are the everlasting arms."[8]

"Living a life of faith," writes Oswald Chambers, "means never knowing where you are being led. But it does mean loving and knowing the One who is leading. It is literally a life of faith, not of understanding and reason — a life of knowing Him who calls us to go."[9]

One of the Enemy's most damaging tactics is to paralyze us with our own emotional and psychological wounds — to fill us with such pain and shame that we despair of ever being able to "get up and walk." Jim Cymbala says,

> Instead of focusing on the faithfulness of God, we focus on what the circumstances seem to dictate. . . . But faith enables us to see God on top of all our problems. If we only see the problems, we get depressed and start making wrong decisions. . . . "Unbelief" talks to itself instead of talking to God . . . when we talk to ourselves, we're not talking to anyone very smart because our outlook is very limited. But if we talk to God, we're talking to someone who knows everything. He knows what He promised in the beginning, and He knows exactly how to fulfill those promises no matter the circumstances.[10]

ISAAC'S QUESTION

A look back at Genesis 22 reminds us of the seemingly precarious circumstances Isaac experienced. After traveling for three long days with his father and two servants to worship God on Mt. Moriah, the time had come to make the sacrifice. His father sprang into action.

"Abraham took the wood for the burnt offering and placed it on his son Isaac, and he himself carried the fire and the knife."[11] That step probably felt quite normal to Isaac. But something was missing. "As the two of them went on together, Isaac spoke up and said to his father Abraham, 'Father?'"[12]

"'Yes, my son?'" Abraham replied.[13]

"'The fire and wood are here,' Isaac said, 'but where is the lamb for the burnt offering?'"[14]

Where is the lamb? The question can be heart-stopping when we realize it even needs to be asked. How many times have you and I been walking through life, assuming that everything is going as we think it should? We are humming in the shower and singing in the rain because life is good and we are experiencing abundance — or at least "normalcy." Then, quite suddenly, an unexpected crisis enters our comfortable little world and we realize something is missing. We turn to our Father God much like Isaac turned to his Father Abraham and we say, "Lord, where is the provision for my need?"

Our questions are numerous:

- Lord, where is the money for the house payment?
- Why did my spouse betray me?
- Why didn't you protect my son/daughter from the drug dealer?
- Why did my coworker get the promotion instead of me?
- Where is the energy to deal with my rebellious children?
- Where is the power to overcome this horrible addiction?
- Why did my friend die of cancer?
- How can I leave behind the only life script I have ever known?
- Lord, why didn't you stop my son from shooting Douglas Miller Jr.?

Isaac's father offered an immediate, clear, and confident response to Isaac's question. "Abraham answered, 'God himself will provide the lamb for the burnt offering, my son.' And the two of them went on together."[15]

The lack of any hesitation in Abraham's answer to Isaac's query amazes me. Abraham already knew *who* the sacrifice would be. God had clearly asked him to offer up Isaac, the son of promise, the son Sarah bore in her old age, the precious son whose name means *laughter.* The drama of that moment — to see my son's innocent eyes looking at me with all of the love and trust a child could offer as he asked about the whereabouts of the lamb — would have taken my breath away. But Abraham answered simply and powerfully: "God himself will provide the lamb for the burnt offering."

Abraham's response is better understood if we read these reflections from the book of Hebrews:

> By faith, Abraham, at the time of testing, offered Isaac back to God. Acting in faith, he was as ready to return the promised son, his only son, as he had been to receive him — and this after he had already been told, "Your descendants shall come from Isaac." Abraham figured that if God wanted to, he could raise the dead. In a sense, that's what happened when he received Isaac back, alive from off the altar.[16]

Abraham's faith was so great that he trusted God to bring Isaac back to life, if he followed God's instructions and sacrificed his son. Abraham had been walking with God long enough that he didn't second-guess the instructions he had been given. He listened. He responded. He kept listening. Can you imagine what would have happened if Abraham had quit listening to God after Isaac was placed on the altar? The son of promise would have been killed. Here is what actually happened:

> When they reached the place God had told him about, Abraham built an altar there and arranged the wood on it. He bound his son Isaac and laid him on the altar, on top of the wood. Then he reached out his hand and took the knife to slay his son. But the angel of the LORD called out to him from heaven, "Abraham! Abraham!"
>
> "Here I am," he replied.
>
> "Do not lay a hand on the boy," he said. "Do not do anything to him. Now I know that you fear God, because you have not withheld from me your son, your only son."
>
> Abraham looked up and there in a thicket he saw a ram caught by its horns. He went over and took the ram and sacrificed it as a burnt offering instead of his son. So Abraham called that place The LORD Will Provide. And to this day it is said, "On the mountain of the LORD it will be provided."[17]

When *the* Thicket Is Empty

The provision of a ram in the thicket seems to represent the answer to fervent prayers, the determined choice to wait upon God, the reward for spiritual obedience, or the predictable result of deep and abiding faith. Delayed or unfulfilled hopes can destroy faith or strengthen faith. But is true faith always dependent upon the provision of whatever the "lamb" represents to us? Is faith more powerful when the lamb appears — or can faith be even greater when the desired outcome doesn't happen?

In the middle of our never-ending ordeal, I went out for lunch with three friends I've known for over a decade. As we sat at a window table in the River Crab Restaurant overlooking the fast-moving waters of the St. Clair River, sunshine enveloped my radiant lunch partners. We were a motley crew, to say the least. A few months earlier Sylvia had lost her precious husband, Larry, to leukemia following a bone marrow transplant, months of living in an apartment near the hospital, and a long, valiant struggle. Marilyn was in pain after multiple surgeries that followed an accident that took place years earlier. She was facing major surgery *again*. I was still in the throws of Jason's horrific and unlikely journey. Nan had stage 4 breast cancer and had recently been told by the doctors that all they could do was manage her pain and give her another round of chemotherapy. All of us needed a ram in the thicket.

Sylvia, Marilyn, Nan, and I have all tried to live our lives to make Jesus smile. We have invested time, money, and high energy in living for things that will last forever, and one of our greatest desires is to glorify God with our choices, our commitments, and our opportunities. *So, Father, where is the lamb?* Where is God's provision for our needs? His "reward" for our obedience? Sylvia's husband died. Marilyn's pain increased. Nan's cancer kept growing. My son was incarcerated. The thicket was empty.

Two months later Gene and I visited Nan in her home. She looked classy in her stylish turban, but I quickly realized her hair had fallen out *again*. As our husbands chatted, she pulled me into the living room and told me she needed to talk to me alone. "Carol," she said, "we've been friends a long time. I don't know how much time I have left. It might be a few weeks or it might be a few months, but unless something miraculous happens, I'm going home to be with Jesus soon." I could hardly see her face because my own eyes were brimming with tears and the pain in my heart was unbearable. "Would you be willing to do the eulogy at my memorial service?"

I burst into tears. I didn't want to upset Nan, but I could not control my emotions. "I-I-I don't know if I could do that," I stammered. "I don't want you to leave us." We were close friends who had shared spiritual victories and deep sorrows. Nan had visited my son at the Orlando jail and prayed with him. She had assisted me in ministry by writing letters of encouragement to people who had read my books and had questions about faith and about how to know God more intimately. I wanted to come through for Nan. My tears continued to gush, but before we left the room, I promised her that I would do the eulogy, with the help of another one of Nan's close friends, my sister, Bonnie.

During the next couple of months Nan grew weaker. One night Gene and I stopped by the house to see how she was doing. A few days earlier, one side of her face collapsed from what might have been a small stroke or palsy. She was seeing four versions of everything out of her left eye, so she wore a patch to keep from getting nauseated from the quadruple vision. We laughed with "Pirate Nan," who was able to bring a touch of humor to this devastating situation, and we talked at length about our children, our passions, and our faith. Nan was calm and relaxed as she said, "I'm totally at peace and I'm ready to be with Jesus."

A few days later I stopped by with flowers and a card. Her birthday was coming up on the weekend. She was too weak to open her eyes or to speak, so I did all of the talking. "I'm really jealous of you, Nan. You are going to heaven before I get there, and you are going to be out of pain and you will see Jesus face-to-face." A glimmer of a smile danced on her lips. I leaned over her bed and took her sweet face in my hands as I kissed her on the forehead. "I love you, Nan Walker." Her words were inaudible, but she mouthed, "I love you."

THE POWER *of* FAITH

Nan's celebration service was the following Wednesday. As my sister and I
gathered material for the eulogy, Bonnie remembered a letter she had received
from Nan after asking if she ever felt angry or bitter over the cancer. Here is
how Nan responded:

> It is interesting you should ask that question. I haven't gotten angry
> or bitter. On several occasions when I've had to give up our dreams
> for the future, I felt forlorn and somewhat depressed, but this was
> temporary. Once I worked through the change of plans, accepted
> reality, and charted a new course, the past became the past. I don't
> dwell on it.
>
> I get angry about injustice. But because I don't look at my can-
> cer as an injustice, I haven't gotten angry. I look at the change in the
> status of my health going from good to bad as something God has
> *entrusted* to me. My hope is that what is happening to me will bring
> glory to God. God is good all the time. He loves me and I know that.
> Whatever is best for me is His plan for me. I don't think I caused
> cancer to take up residence in my body — and God is not punishing
> me for anything I have done. He has something wonderful in store
> for me. I think about what that might be.
>
> I am not ever going to experience death. At the moment, or
> maybe just before I take my last breath, I will be with the Lord —
> *living* with Him for an eternity. When that time comes, God will
> extend His grace to get me through it. I have His strength every
> minute, and I talk to Him all the time. Jesus is right here with me. I
> have joy and peace.

Nan Walker's legacy was her faith — and because of her example, my faith
is stronger. In this lifetime, in spite of powerful prayer and abiding trust in the
God she loved, there was no ram in the thicket. Nevertheless, the absence of an
alternate sacrifice did not diminish Nan's faith. God was still her Jehovah-Jirah,

and He provided everything she needed. Her faith enabled her to see what is unseen but certain — a future in God's eternal embrace.

In my mind, Nan has joined that great gallery of heroes in Hebrews 11, about whom we read:

> I could go on and on, but I've run out of time. There are so many more — Gideon, Barak, Samson, Jephthah, David, Samuel, the prophets . . . Through acts of faith, they toppled kingdoms, made justice work, took the promises for themselves. . . . There were those who, under torture, refused to give in and go free, preferring something better: resurrection. . . . Not one of these people, even though their lives of faith were exemplary, got their hands on what was promised. God had a better plan for us: that their faith and our faith would come together to make one completed whole, their lives of faith not complete apart from ours.[18]

Henry Blackaby says, "To walk faithfully with God will always bring a person to experience God's laying His Heart over his."[19] As we lay our Isaac down without demanding that the thicket produce a ram, we will discover that our Jehovah-Jirah *is* the God who provides. He lays His heart over our heart and holds us tenderly, loving us as we trust Him for what we cannot see.

"There is guidance for each of us," wrote Ralph Waldo Emerson well over 150 years ago. "And by lowly listening, we shall hear the right word. . . . Place yourself in the middle of the stream of power and wisdom which flows into your life. Then, without effort, you are impelled to truth and to perfect contentment. . . . A believing love will relieve us of a vast load of care. Oh, my brothers, God exists!"[20]

In the middle of our endless wait for the trial that never seemed to happen, Judy and Orvey Hampton, friends who had prayed for us almost since the beginning of the ordeal, met us for dinner. After an evening of uplifting conversation, they presented us with a gift that offered another creative way for us to find intimacy and companionship with God, and relief and encouragement for our arduous journey. It was a Bible, with every verse in the Scriptures that deals with *Hope* highlighted. Leafing through the pages, I realized how much time was involved in preparing a gift of this magnitude, and I shed tears of gratefulness for the friends who were standing by us, no matter how long this experience lasted.

When we returned home, this note was in our e-mail box:

Dear Carol and Gene,

What a precious time it was to be with you on Saturday night. On our drive home we could not help but rejoice in the fact that through this incredibly painful time, and seemingly hopeless circumstances, you two are keeping your eyes on the One who is our hope. When I think of the verse in Job 6:10 I think of you two. "But it is still my consolation, and I rejoice in unsparing pain, that I have not denied the words of the Holy One." We both wept a lot on our drive . . . wishing there was something we could DO to help. But, the better thing is to pray, and we do that, knowing *by faith* that He is working, however silently.

Love,

Judy & Orvey

Our visit with these faith-filled friends had lifted our hearts. But even more sustaining was reading the highlighted verses in the Bible they placed in our hands that evening. The comforting words of Scripture helped us realize that God was not judging us or forgetting us. Rather, He was holding us with His presence, providing comfort, clearer vision, and the sustenance we needed for the unknown path ahead.

God's Power in *Your* Circumstances

When life is clicking along routinely it's easy to feel like our faith is intact. When a challenge rises up in our path, we who have had a long-term relationship with God may feel that our faith will surely conquer the challenge, even if we must wait and struggle for a while. But when we're confronted with an Isaac experience — something far beyond where our faith has tread before — we have the opportunity to learn what the essential nature of true Christian faith really is. As we read in the book of Hebrews, "The fundamental fact of existence is that this trust in God, this faith, is the firm foundation under everything that makes life worth living. It's our handle on *what we can't see*."[21] I have found that the greatest power of faith lies not in how we think we might use it to conquer challenges we're sure a loving God would not put in our path, but in how we live — with courage, passion, and purpose — in the midst of unresolved, and sometimes immovable, obstacles.

1. Consider a time when God didn't answer your faith-filled prayers with the obvious "rescuing" intervention you asked Him for. How did you feel? What specific questions about God, faith, life, and yourself were you left with? Has anything you've read in this chapter been helpful in your ongoing experience of processing what you've considered to be an "unhappy ending"?

2. In what area or circumstance do you currently find yourself asking God, "But where is the lamb?" Consider at least three specific needs you have that are not yet being met in obvious ways. List them as pointed questions to God, as on page 126.

3. Reflect on Jim Cymbala's words: "People with faith develop a second kind of sight. They see more than just the circumstances; they see God right beside them." As you look at your current unresolved circumstances, where do you see God in proximity to you? Do you sense His right-beside-you presence? Or is He distant from you or even absent altogether? Get out pen and paper and use precise words and images to describe exactly how your relationship with God looks and feels right now.

4. On page 128 I wrote, "Is faith more powerful when the lamb appears — or can faith be even greater when the desired outcome doesn't happen?" What do *you* think, based on your own experiences?

5. Think of someone you know whose faith has made your own faith stronger. Or consider the elements of Abraham's faith, or my friend

Nan's faith, that most challenge or inspire you in your current Isaac experience. In what specific ways would you like to see your faith change and grow?

6. Consider doing a faith-building project like Judy and Orvey Hampton did for us (see page 131). In a Bible, or through a search command on Bible software, look up every scriptural reference to faith. How could having such a comprehensive reference help you in the days ahead to see and walk by faith in unthinkable circumstances?

chapter seven

EMBRACING THE UPSIDE-DOWN NATURE OF THE CROSS

The Power *of* Joy

In the midst of the sorrows is consolation, in the midst of the darkness is light, in the midst of the despair is hope, in the midst of Babylon is a glimpse of Jerusalem, and in the midst of the army of demons is the consoling angel.

—HENRI NOUWEN

THE MONTH OF APRIL 2002 WAS FAST APPROACHING. WE knew that there was every possibility this trial would be delayed like the last seven had. We also knew a call could come at any time telling us J.P. had been offered a plea bargain. That call did not come. Once again concerned relatives made plans to sit with us in the courtroom during the most intense experience of our lives. The tension was thick. Eerie. Frightening. Life felt surreal.

Gene and I flew into Orlando on Sunday evening and met April at the courthouse where our son would go on trial the next day. The justice complex was massive. It took up an entire city block and was more than twenty stories high. We had made plans with April to do a Jericho-style prayer walk around the complex before jury selection began, for the second time in two-and-a-half years, on Monday morning. The circular trip around that gigantic building took a long time, and we prayed fervently for the judge, the prosecutor, and J.P.'s attorneys. We asked God to protect Jason and to give him strength and wisdom; we prayed for his demeanor in the courtroom and for insight should there be a plea bargain offer even at this late date.

We agonized in prayer over the jury selection process. We pled with God not to allow any member on the jury who would not be His choice. Before flying to Florida earlier that day a mental picture came clearly into my mind. God was seated on a regal, white throne, with clouds all around Him. As I saw Him in all of His power and glory, I envisioned Him as the righteous judge of the universe hovering over the top of the Orlando courthouse. I recognized God as the superintendent of all that would happen in the courthouse during Jason's trial. He was seated on His throne in majesty and splendor, and I believed that *nothing* could happen in the courtroom that was not permitted to happen without His powerful and righteous approval. My faith was big and my hopes were high.

On our final turn around the front of the courthouse we paused at the main entrance to the building. Security devices were in full view just inside the lobby, and I envisioned the key players in J.P.'s trial going through the metal detectors and stepping onto the elevators. Gene, April, and I had been speaking our prayers aloud as we walked, and now we approached the courthouse doors with the same boldness. Security guards immediately stepped forward as our hands reached out to touch the doors. We explained that we were there to pray for a trial that would begin in the building the next day. They rolled their eyes and looked at each other as if to say, "We have some wacky but harmless people here. Let's leave them alone." The three of us laid hands on the gigantic doors and prayed passionately for all of the weighty decisions that would be made inside the building in the days ahead.

THE TRIAL

Looking back on my life, there has been no time period of greater emotional pain than the week of my son's trial for first-degree murder. It lasted for five seemingly endless days. We were told that the *Court TV* cameras would be rolling from the beginning to the end of the trial, and there was nothing we could do legally to stop them. The trial was carried live on the *Court TV* website and later aired in an edited version on *Dateline NBC* on national television. Print media journalists and television reporters tried to get interviews from family members as they entered or exited the courtroom. We knew they were just doing their job, but we were under enough stress without dealing with the media too.

On Monday, April 15, Gene, April, and I had once again been asked by Jason's attorney to be absent from the courtroom during the jury selection process; however, other relatives were allowed inside, and we received periodic updates on how this tedious process was moving forward. With so much at stake, the three of us found the waiting to be a daunting task. The word *wait* means, "to remain stationary in readiness or expectation," or "to look forward expectantly," or "to be ready and available," or "to remain temporarily neglected or unrealized."[1] We were definitely feeling readiness, and our expectations were high regarding what might take place in the courtroom. We looked forward to witnessing the miracle God might perform. He was our merciful, rescuing God! But there were also many moments when we didn't sense God's presence at all, and fear overshadowed hope as we felt neglected by Him.

I wrote in my journal in small blurts. I spent much of my energy just trying to remember to breathe.

> April 15 — The anxiety in the air is so thick I could cut it with a knife. This day is so odd. I find myself doing the same things over and over again. I can't concentrate. I try to pray, but then realize I am already praying for my son, for this trial, and all parties involved with every breath I take. We need resolution, but I am so afraid of resolution.

By the end of the first day, half of the jury members had been selected. That evening the family had dinner together, and we were enveloped in the kind of love that requires no words. With every touch of a hand, during each lingering hug, and through eye contact, we shared our anxiety and unspoken prayers.

Jury selection continued at 9:00 A.M. the next day.

April 16 — It's Tuesday. We did another Jericho walk around the
courthouse last night. Gene, April, and I can't be in the courtroom until after we testify because we are witnesses to J.P.'s mental state prior to the murder. The agony of waiting is excruciating.
J.P. gets picked up at the jail at 4:00 A.M. every morning and
gets taken with other inmates who have their trials this week to
a holding area in the basement of the courthouse. He handed us
a note through Bill Barnett, asking us to pray for the other men
who are in court this week. He's been praying over the men in
the holding area every morning.

By lunchtime on the second day all twelve jurors had been selected.

Bill Barnett knew the agony we were in, and he gave us permission to sit in
the hallway outside the courtroom doors on the third day of the trial. When the
doors closed, we waited . . . and I memorized the stately appearance of the walls,
furnishings, and decor. Hour after hour we sat on formal Chippendale sofas in
that somber place, awaiting the opening of the doors for the midmorning and
afternoon breaks.

The prosecutor had finished presenting her case, and this was the day that
three of the psychiatrists who had interviewed J.P. would take the stand. The
testimony of these men could determine our son's future. A heaviness engulfed
me like a thick, dark cloud of oppression.

Fortunately I had brought with me a three-ring binder that had been sent
by my intercessor friend, Kathy Blume. She and many of our Stretcher Bearers
had been on a forty-day prayer vigil in preparation for the trial. The caption
on the front cover said, "Prayer Changes Things." Opening the book, I read
Kathy's handwritten words:

These scriptures, quotes, and prayers have been compiled during our
prayer vigil for your family. Our hearts have been turned toward a
HOLY GOD who has penetrated our own hearts as we have been on
our faces for each of you. The fragrance of our worship is permeating
heaven and our ABBA FATHER has heard. *Glory, Glory, Glory,* to the

Lord God Almighty. . . . You are loved. We are embracing what God
has arranged.

During the next several hours I read, sometimes silently, sometimes aloud
to April and Gene, the many letters from friends and relatives who had sent
their support, encouragement, and prayers for the week of the trial. There were
pictures of our praying family members and friends on the pages next to their
letters. Mother and Dad Afman (my parents) sent a copy of a verse I had memorized as a child: "Don't worry about anything; instead, pray about everything;
tell God your needs and don't forget to thank Him for His answers. If you do
this, you will know God's peace, which is far more wonderful than the human
mind can understand. His peace will keep your thoughts and your hearts quiet
and at rest, as you trust in Christ Jesus."[2] Focusing on God's Word helped to
keep me from coming completely unglued during the interminable wait.

Before we left the building that evening, the three of us were informed we
would be called to testify the next day. That night I wrestled over what to wear in
the courtroom. As a professional speaker, I was often dressed in a suit and heels,
but I wondered if that look would make me appear to be an affluent mother
trying to rescue her son. This was Florida. Many women here didn't even wear
hosiery — just sandals. While I knew the case rested in God's hands, I wanted to
do my part to help my son. The issue wasn't really clothing, of course.

April 17 — My heart feels like it's doing cartwheels in my chest. What
    if I say the wrong things? What if I hurt my son's chances for a
    favorable verdict? Time feels like it's standing still, but simultane-
    ously it's rushing so fast I can't keep up. I can't sleep. I can't eat.

I agonized long into the night. When my head finally hit the pillow, I
curled up next to Gene, seeking the comfort of human touch. We clung to each
other and prayed for our son.

The next morning, very few words passed between Gene, April, and me as
we prepared to leave for the courthouse. We each had our own heartache but
tried to carry the weight of the pain for each other. April looked pretty in a navy

blue sailor dress with a big white collar. Her long brunette locks fell past her shoulders, outlining her tiny frame. April's hands were ice cold, and she said she felt sick.

We met family members at the courthouse and embraced each other. Another psychiatrist was on the stand in the morning, so once again, we waited in the hallway. During the midmorning break, I was in the ladies' room when Dorothy Sedgwick walked out of one of the stalls. Both the prosecutor and I were startled. For a moment our eyes met — two women, both of us mothers. She, arguing to convict my son of first-degree murder, and me, desperately praying that she would understand that my son was not thinking clearly and had acted on the conviction that he was protecting two little girls. *Surely*, I thought, *she would see that the defendant she was prosecuting was from a good family and that he had a strong base of support. The law is the law, but did J.P. need to be locked up for the rest of his life in order to protect our society?* I opened my mouth, but it was difficult to form words. "G-g-g-good morning," I stammered. The prosecutor nodded, without facial expression, and moved on.

During the lunch hour, Bill Barnett met with us in the hallway to give us the order of our appearances on the witness stand. Gene would be first, followed by April, and I would testify last. It was an afternoon that is forever frozen in time in my mind. The three of us prayed together and clutched each other's hands. Then Gene was called and he disappeared through the heavy courtroom doors. An hour later he emerged, and I could see the impact of the stress on his face and in his demeanor.

April was called next and my mother's heart wished I could hold her in my arms while she went through the verbal beating from the prosecutor. With twenty years of experience, Dorothy Sedgwick had finely honed her skill of asking questions in such a way that a witness could quickly appear confused, intimidated, unsure, and even self-contradictory. This is what happened when April was questioned relentlessly about the past physical and sexual abuse she alleged against her ex-husband. She was pounded and humiliated, and her personal integrity seemed to be on trial that day more than the actions of J.P. Following her testimony she came out the door hurt, exhausted, baffled, and beaten. She was afraid she had only hurt her husband's case.

I later heard from a certified Victim Advocate who had seen April's testimony on *Dateline NBC*. The woman had worked with sexual abuse victims
for years in both church and correctional facility settings. "It shocked me," she
wrote, "that no one in the courtroom seemed to realize that April was having
trouble with consistent recall of events because of past trauma. Why didn't your
lawyer call any experts who understood how the trauma of abuse affects victims
and how they can come across as witnesses?" I had no answer.

I was the final witness of the day. After making my oath to tell the truth, I
took the stand. J.P. was at the table to my right. My eyes flooded with tears and
a huge lump formed in my throat. Our eyes met and I mouthed, "I love you." I
knew he understood. I looked at the judge and briefly glanced at the jury. These
people would decide the fate of our son. My fear was great.

During the next hour I responded to a battery of questions about my son's
emotional and mental state prior to the crime, his obsessive fear that Chelsea
and Hannah would be harmed if their father got unsupervised visitation, and
his impeccable record and compassionate acts of kindness to others prior to this
horrific event. After the prosecutor grilled me, the defense rested.

> April 18 — Okay, now I feel like I'm coming unglued. One by one we
> were called to the stand — first Gene, then April, and finally, me.
> I prayed to find kind eyes in the courtroom. The questions were
> first from Bill Barnett, then from the prosecutor. I hated this
> experience. It was surreal to see my son behind the defendant's
> table. It was like watching a TV show, only I knew all of the play-
> ers. As I left the courtroom, I knew I should have done a better
> job. I second-guessed my responses for the rest of the day.

We knew that closing arguments would be delivered to the jury the next
day. On every night of the trial we had done Jericho-style prayer walks around
the perimeter of the courthouse. Thursday night's walk was particularly emotional, because we knew a huge decision would be made very soon.

On Friday we awakened early, exhausted.

April 19 — It's April's birthday, but we won't be celebrating. Closing
arguments will be made before noon. My breath comes in short,
labored puffs. I wonder if it's possible to run out of tears.

We drove downtown and met family and friends outside the courtroom
door. Dr. Joel Hunter, J.P. and April's pastor, and his wife, Becky, came to pray
with the family and to be with us during the closing arguments. The courtroom
was crowded with people, cameras, jury members, and attorneys. I felt overwhelmed, yet keenly aware that an army of praying friends all over the country
was covering the court proceedings that would take place on the seventh floor of
the Orlando courthouse that day. For a moment, a flash of joy came over me as I
realized that the long wait would soon be over. Surely we were about to witness
a miracle of mercy and grace!

Judge Lauten called us to order. Closing statements were presented — first
by the prosecutor, then by the defense attorney, followed by the prosecutor once
again. The jury members were given their instructions. We were dismissed for
lunch, then began a long afternoon of waiting while the jury was sequestered.
We determined to make good use of our time, so that afternoon we did seven
Jericho-style prayer walks around the courthouse, praying for each member of
the jury, pleading with God on behalf of our son.

By late afternoon all of the attorneys, family members, and friends, along
with the media representatives had gathered in the waiting area outside the
courtroom. The tension was palpable. Some people sat on the furniture and
held hands while they intermittently talked and prayed. Others sat on the floor.
At about 5:00 P.M. we were told to come back into the courtroom. The jury had
a question. We thought that might be a good sign, but it was about a technicality
on the verdict form. The foreman of the jury asked their question; they left, and
once again we were dismissed. Tension mounted. At 5:30 P.M. we were called
back into the courtroom. The verdict was in.

We took our seats and held each other's hands as we silently prayed. The
twelve men and women had reached a unanimous verdict. A piece of paper was
handed to the judge. Jason was asked to stand and the verdict was calmly read:

"We, the jury, find the defendant, Jason Paul Kent, guilty of murder in the first degree."

I was stifling sobs. April's head was in her lap and she was rocking back and forth with grief. Gene's neck and face were red, and the anguish of a father in pain was on full display. The jury was polled. Then Jason was asked to stand before the judge for his sentencing. We already knew what the sentence would be. Since the maximum possible sentence — death — had already been taken off the table by the prosecutor's office, the minimum possible sentence for first-degree murder would automatically be imposed in accordance with Florida state law. The judge could not deliberate and suggest an alternative number of years based on his own judgment or the circumstances of the case. So, in a swift, heart-stopping moment, Judge Lauten delivered a brief statement to Jason, ending with, "I hereby sentence you to life in prison, without the possibility of parole."

There are moments in our lives when we can't think. We simply feel the pain, the heartache, the brokenness, and the sorrow. That was my experience for a few minutes. Then everything felt like it was whirling in slow motion. I looked at the judge and wondered if he believed the verdict was fair and appropriate. My eyes swept over the faces of the members of the jury. I looked at the straight back of Dorothy Sedgwick and wondered, *What is she feeling right now? Happy? Nothing?* I glanced at Bill Barnett and Bert Barclay. Jason's attorneys were not used to losing. I wondered, *Was this just another case to them, or did they truly care about Jason? Do they care what this is doing to our family?* I looked at my son, child of my womb, and wondered if he would be tormented by suicidal thoughts after receiving a sentence with no hope of release — ever. What would happen to my boy?

The verdict and the sentencing came down on April Kent's twenty-eighth birthday. I could not fathom why God allowed this. It felt hurtful, even malicious. My daughter-in-law was in deep grief. And so was I.

> The trial is finally over. We lost. On April's birthday. For the rest
> of her life she will be reminded of the sadness of April 19, when she
> should be celebrating a fresh year of her life. This is beyond cruel,
> God. I want to pound my fists at You to express my anger and

extreme disappointment in You, but I don't know how to find You. Are you even listening to me?

My spirit is groaning with grief and pain. I have never felt such a depth of mourning. I'm not sure I can continue to live. I wonder if people ever die from a broken heart.

A TOE-TAG SENTENCE

Jason stood, as if at attention, as he nodded to the judge, acknowledging that he heard the sentence. Handcuffs and the waist chain were immediately placed on him. As he was ushered out of the courtroom our son's eyes met ours for a moment of shared agony, grief, and love. The anguish was too enormous for my heart to hold.

Our family and friends gathered on the far side of the hallway outside the courtroom to weep together. My body shook and my heart felt like it was alternately skipping a beat and then doing calisthenics in my chest cavity. The reporters were lurking in the shadows, hoping for a word from the grieving parents. They angered me, but I was in too much grief to express hostility. We spent a half hour alternately sobbing in the arms of Jason's grandparents, holding on to our family members, thanking friends for standing with us, and mumbling final words to the attorneys, "Thank you for trying."

J.P. had been given a "toe-tag" sentence. In the common legal and prison vernacular, that means you received a sentence so severe that the only way you will ever leave prison is on a slab with a tag on your toe, indicating that you are deceased. Our son, now only twenty-seven years old, without any prior record of any kind, had been sentenced to life, without the possibility of parole — *ever*.

As we left the courthouse, we were still in shock. Our extended family members went back to their hotel, and Gene and I drove back to April's home. Gene knew his parents were in deep grief, so he went to be with them. April and I felt like we were walking in a valley so black and deep that we couldn't imagine ever getting out of it. The family had asked if we wanted to join them, but we didn't have the energy or the courage to be with a group of people. We alternately wept, clung to each other, and grieved for J.P.

An hour later we heard a knock at the door. It was my precious mother and my sister Bonnie. They walked in and we fell into each other's arms, weeping. They said, "We knew if we called that you would say you couldn't be with people tonight; but we *know* you need to be with us tonight; so we're here, and we're *staying*."

We experienced the comfort of companionship. Mama and Bonnie wept with us, prayed with us, and held us in their arms. April was in deep sorrow, and I was a broken woman, acutely aware that in spite of multiple Jericho prayer walks around the courthouse and hundreds of people praying for us all over the country, God had not answered our prayers in the way we had hoped. We shared very few words that night. Mama sat in the rocking chair and Bonnie and I walked April over to the sofa. My sister sat at the end of the couch and began to massage April's feet. Mama stroked her face with her soft, Dutch hands. I poured some lotion in my hands and massaged April's shoulders, arms, and hands. It was a night I will never forget. Gut-wrenching pain. Shared sorrow. A personal Good Friday experience that seemed to offer no promise of resurrection.

But God didn't abandon us to that pitch-dark despair. In the "Prayer Changes Things" notebook that Kathy Blume put together was a note from my friend, Lael Arrington. Just the day before I had read the verse she had wanted me to meditate on during this horrific week: "He will cover you with his feathers, and under his wings you will find refuge; his faithfulness will be your shield and rampart."[3] Lael also wrote:

> Every private family matter that is revealed, every tender place in
> your heart and April's heart that gets probed and poked through this
> whole ordeal, God will cover, softly and soothingly, and provide the
> refuge you need. And the whole ordeal and your faithfulness through
> it will be a finger pointing others to a God who is softer and more
> tender, stronger and more protecting. The lamb-like Lion . . . The
> lion-like Lamb.

One manifestation of this promise came on Tuesday morning following the verdict. A package arrived at April's house that was addressed to Gene, April, and me. Someone had overnighted a box from Phoenix that was filled with soft Kleenex tissues in all sizes and in April's favorite colors — shades of lavender and light purple. Under the tissues were scented candles in the same colors. The note was brief.

> Dear Ones,
> We are praying that you will feel God wrapping His arms around you in this time of unspeakable grief. Please know how much you are loved.
>
> Rich and Kathe Wunnenberg

Opening that package was like burrowing into the soft feathers of a mother hen as she covered us with her love and protection. Rich and Kathe knew we didn't need a sermon on how to overcome our suffering. We needed a safe place to cry. We needed a sense of protection during this most vulnerable time of our lives.

THIS ISN'T *the* LIFE I PRAYED FOR

Earlier in our journey I had often struggled with depression that would creep in during the late afternoon or early evening hours. But I made a surprising discovery. Most mornings, when the sun came up, I experienced renewed hope and a surprising sense of joy.

How very dark Good Friday must have been for those who loved and followed Jesus! He had been given a sentence even more severe, only He was without sin. Jesus was perfect in every way, yet He came to this earth as a babe with a "toe-tag" sentence. He was born to die. He had a hopeless case before He even entered the world. When Jesus died on the cross on that Good Friday over two thousand years ago, joy and hope were ripped from His followers' hearts. They had believed He would be the One who would redeem Israel from the oppression of the Romans. Now His body was in a tomb. It certainly looked like He'd received a toe-tag sentence.

But I'm convinced that when the sun rose on that first Easter morning and revealed an empty tomb, joy replaced the sadness and darkness. In the middle of bleak circumstances, Christ's resurrection reminds us that joy can return. The psalmist proclaims, "Weeping may go on all night, but joy comes with the morning."[4]

Joy. What is this elusive emotion? The dictionary says it is "intense happiness or great delight, that which gives rise to this emotion, or on which the emotion centers."[5] As I dug deeper into the authentic reasons for this celebratory response, I realized that the key to understanding authentic joy is in *knowing that which gives rise to what the emotion is centered on.* Joy often brings a smile to the face, a lightness to the step, and an anticipation that our lives will be blessed with good experiences, agreeable people, and enough money to cover our expenses. But that isn't always what joy looks like. If our focus is centered on the sadness in this world, the hopelessness of our circumstances, the unspeakable pain we are in, then we will experience endless sorrow and relentless grief. So the key to joy for Christians who willingly lay their Isaac down must be in understanding the upside-down nature of the cross. We do not grieve as those who have no hope.[6]

My friend Cathy lost her job for the second time within a year. She is educated, attractive, hardworking, and dedicated to God. She's also a single woman with rent and bills to pay. In a note not long ago she wrote,

> To me the resurrection means having God's joy inside me no matter what's going on outside me. When I think of the events leading to the resurrection — Jesus' beatings, crucifixion, and slow, torturous death — I remember that as I wait for the right job to surface, I must crucify any negative or angry thoughts and words, and resurrect them as God's peaceful, joyful alternatives.

Cathy understands the power of joy and the upside-down nature of the cross.

Another friend named Kathy was filled with hopes, dreams, and a deep desire to be a godly woman when she was a young university student. She longed to find a life partner with a passion for God — a man of integrity who would cherish her and live out his faith. When she met and eventually married Ron, she believed he was her one true love. Her story did not unfold the way she expected.

For the first eight years of our marriage, I was treated with love and respect. I was optimistic that our marriage would be happy, that it would reflect biblical principles, and that we would be a positive example to others.

After my husband took a prestigious coaching job, things changed. He became withdrawn, cold, and indifferent. His nerves were on edge, and he projected all of his anger and rage onto me. In connection with his job, he began drinking heavily and began having multiple affairs. He would come home in the middle of the night, awaken me, and scream false accusations.

During this time we found out our third son was profoundly deaf. Instead of this crisis drawing our family together, Ron was absent from the house even more and became emotionally detached from me and from our sons. I went to my pastor, desperate for help, and he said, "If a man strays from home and begins excessive drinking, it could be that he's unhappy at home. So Kathy, you need to go home and put on your prettiest nightie and wait for him to come home." After receiving that ridiculous advice, I made a vow not to talk to anyone about the problems in my marriage and in my home.

Eventually I got a restraining order and called the police because of Ron's actions toward me and toward our deaf son. I tried to respond according to biblical principles. I longed for my husband to come back to the Lord, and I gave him numerous opportunities to change his behavior. But I had come to fear the man who gave life to my children. At night his irrational violence would often explode. I never wanted a divorce, but my years as a joy-filled bride had turned into a living nightmare. I had three children to protect, and divorce became my only option. When our marriage ended, I had nine dollars in my pocket and no money in the bank.

I was totally unprepared for the negative response from the Christians in my life. It was made quite clear that I was expected to step down from a leadership position in the Bible study I taught. Long-time friends rejected me, and I soon learned that many churches would not allow me to minister to their women because I was divorced. I was shunned.

Over time I heard God asking me to lay down what I had fervently hoped for — redemption for my marriage — and exchange it for whatever He had in mind for me now. Would I let go of the feelings of betrayal and release the anger that God had given me a special-needs child and two active older boys with no husband to model godly masculinity for them?

Even while questioning God, I pressed into Him, maintaining time in the Bible, listening to inspirational music, and exploring old classic Christian books, searching for answers on how to remain faithful in the middle of joyless and hopeless circumstances. I finally gave my broken, confused, and grieving heart to God.

On the day my divorce was final, one of my dear friends died of cancer at the age of forty-one. We had known each other since seventh grade. Early in our marriage, Bob and Pat and Ron and I often got together as friends. They had two sons and we had three. In the months after my divorce and following Pat's death, Bob and I occasionally got our children together. Our boys were friends and we were friends. Time passed. Neither of us was looking for another spouse, but God had a different idea. We were friends, falling in love. Bob's boys needed a mom, and my sons needed a dad.

We each brought our own baggage to a new marriage and learned to "lay it down," slowly at first, and then more quickly as trust grew. Joy returned to my soul — but it's a different kind of joy than I experienced as a young newlywed. It's a bittersweet joy seasoned with pain, betrayal, grief, and rejection; but it's also a deeper joy, based on faith and trust in a resurrected Jesus, the One who understands Good Friday experiences better than anyone else.

SUNRISE

"He (Jesus) was willing to die a shameful death on the cross because of the *joy* he knew would be his afterward. Now he is seated in the place of highest honor beside God's throne in heaven."[7] Jesus died a horrible death and He was placed in a tomb. But Easter morning arrived. When Mary Magdalene and Mary, Martha's sister, visited Jesus' grave that morning, they discovered that God's angel had rolled back the stone. They saw an empty tomb. The angel spoke, "I know you're looking for Jesus, the One they nailed to the cross. He is not here. He was raised, just as he said.... Now get on your way quickly and tell his disciples, 'He is risen from the dead.'"[8]

If I thought for a moment that there was no heaven, no end to my grief, no hope for my son's future, no end to sorrow, I would be tempted to "check out" right now. But Jesus' resurrection turns my personal Good Friday into the hope of Easter Sunday, even if my joy is not fully realized in this life. The good news of the resurrection is what the upside-down nature of the cross is all about. The fact that "He is risen" brings *abiding* joy, not just momentary celebration.

Dr. Larry Crabb writes in his book *Shattered Dreams*:

Our shattered dreams are never random. They are always a piece in a larger puzzle, a chapter in a larger story. Pain is a tragedy. But it's never only a tragedy. For the Christian, it's always a necessary mile on the long journey to joy.

The suffering caused by shattered dreams must not be thought of as something to relieve if we can, or endure if we must. It's an opportunity to be embraced, a chance to discover our desire for the highest blessing God wants to give us, an encounter with Himself...

The journey to joy takes us through shattered dreams ... A new way to live is available to us, a way that leads to a joy-filled encounter with Christ, to a life-arousing community with others, and to a powerful transformation of our interior worlds that makes us more like Jesus.[9]

Could this mean that God is doing something even grander than what I prayed for on the Jericho walks around the courthouse? Is it possible that this agonizing experience is deepening my desire for God, because He's all I have? Is He giving me a new song, a different opportunity, an enlarged territory for doing kingdom work because His plan is far beyond what I was praying for? Will He transform my heartache into joy? Will He give my son purpose and meaning in his life? Do I have a God good enough and big enough to do all this? I have heard it said that either God is everything or He is nothing. The journey from here would show me what I really believed and where my hope really lay.

My own birthday was two days after my son was sentenced. The following day I was finally able to sit down and write a personal e-mail to our entire Stretcher Bearer family. They had already been informed of the verdict.

Dear Stretcher Bearers:

I can't find a word to describe the past week. We are numb with pain and grief — and, at times, overcome by waves of hopelessness. We can only believe by faith that God has a bigger plan than what we can see for J.P. With the network of friends and family across the country who have been praying, we know this judgment is not a mistake.

Usually when a sentence of this magnitude is given, an inmate is put on suicide watch, with his clothes removed, and he's in an isolated area. But J.P. showed total peace when the sentence was read and he was taken back to the faith-based cell block, where he preached at the chapel service within a couple of hours of his sentencing. The other inmates were very depressed, saying that if a man like J.P. got a sentence like this, there is absolutely no hope for them. God allowed him to minister to those men powerfully as he preached.

An hour or so later, J.P. was permanently removed from the Christian cell and placed in the Capital Life area. Usually there is much violence in that cell block, but J.P. called yesterday and said he has a Christian roommate, and this particular cell is much less violent than the other Capital Life cells. He will probably remain at the

Orlando jail for one to two weeks. Then he'll be taken to the reception center for testing before being transferred to his first prison location. When he goes to the reception center, it may take as long as six weeks before he is placed in a prison, and during that time he will not be able to call or write to us or April. We will have no word from him until after he arrives at a prison.

Gene and I were allowed to have a noncontact visit with J.P. last night for about an hour and a half. It was a precious time of grieving together, listening to his concerns for April and the girls, and of purposing together that we will not waste this unexpected opportunity J.P. will have to display the power of God in a difficult place.

You probably know that the verdict came on April's birthday. My birthday was yesterday. Without our knowledge, Stretcher Bearers sent special love gifts. We were in such grief, there was no way we could have a birthday party, so my sister and mother invited us to their hotel room on Saturday and had "an encouragement gathering" with the family members who remained in Orlando. With tears and hugs we read your cards and opened your gifts. Never have we felt so loved, so protected by prayer. We are so weak and broken, but we feel "carried" by a power not our own. Without knowing what the verdict would be, you wrote us remarkable notes, so fitting, so comforting. We received the exquisite bouquet of flowers and the generous gift certificate for food for the family members who were in Florida, and we realized once again what a treasure we have in family and friends. You have walked this road with us for two-and-a-half years, and we are so grateful. It will be impossible for us to write to each of you individually in the next few weeks to thank you properly for your generosity, your encouragement, and your love, but please know how much you mean to us.

Gene and I have claimed this Scripture from 2 Corinthians 4:16-18: "Therefore we do not lose heart. Though outwardly we are wasting away, yet inwardly we are being renewed day by day. For our light and momentary troubles are achieving for us an eternal glory that far out-weighs them all. So we fix our eyes not on what is seen, but on what is unseen. For what is seen is temporary, but what is unseen is eternal."

Lord Jesus, come quickly. Perhaps His coming will be today!

One of the first people who contacted us via e-mail following the sentencing was our friend Debbie. She has known Jason since he was a little boy and watched him grow up. She cheered for him when he was accepted into the U.S. Naval Academy and attended Parent's Weekend with us following his extremely challenging plebe summer.

Debbie viewed the verdict and sentencing on the *Court TV* website, and God led her to intercede for J.P. for the next several hours following that devastating news. J.P. is a lover of adventure and enjoys hiking and mountain climbing, so the message Debbie sent was particularly significant to us:

I have felt like a rope holder. When I was a freshman at Colorado College I joined the mountain climbing club. Before you are allowed to start climbing, they teach you how to be a "rope holder" for another climber, providing a lifeline, if needed. When you see a climber going up or down a mountain face, you usually see the rope tied around his/her waist, but what you often don't see is the person at the end of that rope. It wasn't until I started climbing that I realized the importance of the person who holds your rope while you are climbing . . . your life is literally in their hands if something should happen while you are climbing.

As you and Gene and April and J.P. scaled that mountain this week, there were a multitude of rope holders each day, holding on to your ropes and providing a safety net of prayer. Now, even though the trial is over, I know the climb continues, and this is one rope holder who plans to stay in place as long as there is a climber on the mountain.

In the first hours and days following the sentencing, Gene, April, and I were so weak, exhausted, and immobilized with personal pain that we had difficulty praying, communicating with people, or holding our own heads up. But God has a plan for His broken people — and that plan is for the body of Christ to be their rope holders. They speak up with confident prayers when we cannot move our lips. They allow us to cry, vent our naked feelings, or they mourn with us in solitude. Rope holders stay on the mountain even when they are exhausted in order to provide a safety net. Debbie's words were the living embodiment of Paul's admonition to the early Christians: "Carry each other's burdens, and in this way you will fulfill the law of Christ."[10]

THE POWER *of* JOY

Chelsea and Hannah had spent the week of the trial with a good friend of J.P. and April. They returned home on Sunday, and I noticed that Hannah had no eyelashes. Both of the girls have big brown eyes that sparkle with the enthusiasm of youth, so the missing eyelashes were easy to spot.

It was good to have our seven- and ten-year-old granddaughters back in the house with their mom and us. They didn't understand the full impact of the trial, and they certainly didn't comprehend anything about the depth of grief that filled our hearts. They were just two little girls being themselves, complete with giggles, playing dress-up, and planning tea parties. Fresh hope walked into the house with their unaffected authenticity and boundless energy.

When I asked April about Hannah's missing eyelashes, she explained that when Auntie Amber had visited several months earlier, she told the girls that when an eyelash falls out, you're supposed to make a wish on it and blow it into the air — and when you do that, the wish is supposed to come true. It was simply a playful comment during a visit much earlier on our journey. But Hannah had taken that thought to heart, and without anyone noticing she had started pulling her eyelashes out and wishing that Daddy J.P. would come home from the jail.

It made me weep to hear those words, but it also warmed my heart. As I tucked the girls in one night, I prayed with Chelsea and listened to her sweet petitions for her mommy and daddy. Then I tucked Hannah in. "Grammy," she said, "why aren't grown-ups ever afraid?"

"Oh, we are," I said, "but sometimes we cover it up a little too much."

It had only been a few days since the trial ended, but I found a surprising joy spreading its wings like a butterfly within my soul. These little granddaughters were helping to heal my heart when I held them in my arms. Their spontaneity and pleasure at being in my presence was like a balm, soothing me with renewed hope and resurrected faith. What I would have lost if J.P. had not married April! I had a long way to go to find the true meaning of the upside-down nature of the cross — but part of my cup of joy in the middle of experiencing what felt like a bottomless well of sorrow was being "Grammy" to Chelsea and Hannah. They took my hands in their hands and began leading me in the direction of joy. And Hannah's eyelashes grew back, healthier and thicker than ever before.

On a recent run to Taco Bell with Hannah, I asked her what she wanted to be when she grew up. Without hesitation she said, "I'd like to be a movie star so I could make a million bucks."

"And what would you do with all that money?" I asked.

Her reply came quickly, "I'd buy me a Hummer!" she exclaimed.

"And what would you do with a Hummer?" I queried.

"Oh, Grammy, I'd pick up all of the lost and hurt dogs and I'd take care of them."

I smiled as I pondered her joy in caring for the needs of a vehicle filled with needy dogs and realized how similar our stories really are. During this impossible journey, our entire family has been cared for by our Stretcher Bearers, and the natural response to receiving that much love is to do the same for others in need.

But the admonition found in the book of Hebrews remains our brightest north star: "[Let us fix] our eyes on Jesus, the pioneer and perfecter of faith. For the joy set before him he endured the cross, scorning its shame, and sat down at the right hand of the throne of God."[11] Michael Card puts it this way:

Could the experts from the temple have ever conceived of a God who would endure the cross, scorning the shame of it, for *joy*? I don't think so. Could the soldiers and passersby that day have guessed it from the condition of Christ's body? Never. Did the criminals who hung on either side of Jesus sense it, even just a little? One of them, perhaps . . .

I wonder: What was it about the "joy set before Him" that literally allowed Jesus to scorn the mockery? It certainly didn't prevent Him from experiencing every nerve ending of pain and hours of humiliation. Yet He endured — for the *joy.* Jesus could rise above the mockery of the moment because He soared on the wings of eternal truth.[12]

That is the upside-down nature of the cross. When my son was arrested and eventually convicted of first-degree murder, I was humiliated, embarrassed, and ashamed. I believed I was a failure as a mother. Looking back, so much of my journey was about *my* pain, *my* hurt, *my* reputation, *my* devastation. Only when I began to look at my unthinkable circumstances through the lens of Jesus' death and resurrection did I experience a joy that transcends my heartache.

Now, two years later, some days I start to slip into that deep valley of despair where new life appears unrealizable. But I continue to learn, day by day, that there is no situation, no obstacle, that Christ's resurrection doesn't give me the power to overcome. Whether it's divorce we face, or unemployment, cancer, depression, relationship disasters, fear of terrorism, or living with the knowledge that a beloved son has a "toe-tag" sentence, I'm discovering that Henri Nouwen was right: "The cup of sorrow, inconceivable as it seems, is also the cup of joy. Only when we discover this in our own life can we consider drinking it."[13]

Emily Dickinson was one of my favorite poets during my high-school years. She once said, "Hope is a thing with feathers that perches in the soul and sings the tune without the words and never stops at all." I finally understand what she meant. Jason is still in prison with a hopeless sentence. But in the midst of my tears (which continue to come at unexpected times), when I can't speak inspirational words because my pain is too intense, I know there is a joy in my soul and a hope that rises within my heart. I can't explain it; but it's there. Because Christ rose from the dead, *something more is coming.* Whether my son is locked up for life or he one day walks in freedom, I will choose unshakable faith in unthinkable circumstances.

God's Power in *Your* Circumstances

I have always liked to focus on the "happy" parts of Scripture and of life. Normally I would much prefer reading one of Paul's joyfully confident affirmations over contemplating the psalmists' angst, Job's despair, or Jeremiah's laments — or even Jesus' cries of human desperation. But as I have walked through the dark valley of sorrow, despair, and heart sacrifice, I have drawn some of my greatest comfort from knowing that others have walked through before me — and found redemption, consolation, and even joy in the midst of unthinkable circumstances. I would certainly prefer to live in a state of perpetual Easter celebration, but laying my Isaac down inevitably involves moments of Good Friday desolation. I am glad to know I am in good company.

1. Is *joy* an emotion you tend to experience regularly? Often? Rarely? Never? Has your experience of joy through the years been more the "celebratory" or "abiding" form? On a scale from 0 to 10, where would you say you are right now in terms of experiencing joy? What do you find yourself thinking about as you answer these questions? Where are you placing your focus?

2. Are you living more closely to "Good Friday" or "Easter Sunday"? Read and meditate on the full account of Jesus' last hours on earth in Matthew 26:17–28:20. What, specifically, do you notice in this account of Jesus' personal anguish, death, and resurrection that has the potential to unleash the full power of joy in the midst of your current circumstances?

3. How do you respond to Dr. Larry Crabb's words on page 150: "The journey to joy takes us through shattered dreams"? Has this been your experience, or does the whole idea make you angry? Frightened? Sad? Write out a gut-level-honest prayer to God, telling Him exactly how you feel about the suffering He allows you and those you love to experience. Write until you have nothing more to say, and notice if you experience any shifts of energy or perspective as you pour out your heart to God on paper.

4. Review the Scriptures referred to in this chapter. Choose the one that means the most to you right now and write it on an index card. Meditate on it and memorize it in the week ahead, asking God to use His Word to infuse you with supernatural and abiding joy.

5. On page 154 I wrote: "God has a plan for His broken people — and that plan is for the body of Christ to be their rope holders." How have you experienced this part of God's plan in your own life, past or current? In what specific ways have "rope holders" provided a safety net for you during your darkest hours?

6. Do you know someone who is currently experiencing intense grief or heartache? If so, consider something concrete you can do to give that individual or family a taste of your love and God's comfort, like Rich and Kathe Wunnenberg did when they sent us a timely care package.

chapter eight

FINDING OUR PURPOSE IN GOD'S GRAND STORY

The Power *of* Speaking Up

To live by grace means to acknowledge my whole life story, the light side and the dark. In admitting my shadow side I learn who I am and what God's grace means.

—BRENNAN MANNING

DURING THE NEXT FEW DAYS, THE RELATIVES LEFT ORLANDO and we knew we were entering a different phase of our journey. We needed to begin work on an appeal. There were major financial considerations and legal decisions to make. April and the girls needed to move closer to wherever Jason was placed. Somehow we had to figure out how to go on with life. *What does that cliché mean?* I wondered to myself. *There is no "going on with life." What life? It's a mess.* In my journal I wrote:

It will never be possible for me to answer the question, "What is the greater tragedy? Douglas Miller Jr.'s murder or Jason Kent's life without parole sentence?" There are no winners in this tragedy. We are all losers. Big-time losers. Douglas Miller Sr. and his family lost their son/brother to a violent death. We have lost our son to prison. April has lost her husband to a lifetime in prison. Chelsea and Hannah have lost their biological father, and they have lost their stepfather to prison. We are all total losers. We are all in pain. I don't know who suffers the most and that's not really the point. We are all in horrific places of hurt, shame, guilt, ugliness, and sickening nausea. There are days when I hate my life. Then there are days when I think God can redeem some of the filthy scum of this unspeakable horror.

My only brother calls occasionally, but he rarely writes. Early in our journey he took the time to send me a note, which included a timely reminder that proved critical to my perspective:

Dear Carol,

I am thankful for what you have been for others, including me. But I am most thankful that I know you will allow God to be victorious as you surrender your will to His. You gave J.P. to the Lord before he was born, and you must/will surrender him again into His waiting arms, entrusting J.P. to His care. I pray that you will be able to say, as Jesus did, "Not my will, but Thine be done." Remember, the battle is actually over. We are the only ones who don't know the results. If we trust in Him, if J.P. trusts in Him, the victory is already won!

I love you.

Ben

Chad VanSomeren was the best man at J.P. and April's wedding and J.P.'s roommate at the U.S. Naval Academy. He is a brilliant young officer in the Marine Corps, and Chad always chooses his words carefully. When a note arrived following Jason's conviction and sentencing, it included a verse that had been very meaningful to Gene years earlier when he was a young Christian trying to figure out the ways of God. "Shall not the Judge of all the earth do right?"[1] Chad's note was a reminder that there will always be mysteries in our lives, but the sovereign Judge of the Universe is not limited by our lack of understanding and finite perspective.

I believe that the faith of most of our family and friends remained as strong as it was before the verdict was read. People of faith realize that Jason's trial is only one chapter in the book of his life. Many more chapters will be written, and the Master Editor will "cut and paste, add and delete" many times as He works this tangled script. Ben and Chad reminded me of one thing I know—only because I have read to the end of the Bible. We win. Jesus wins. Gene and I win. J.P., April, Chelsea, and Hannah win. We may not "win" in the way some people would measure a win. But we still win. That means we can, horrifically painful as it is, find meaning in our own Isaac experiences.

Gene journaled after the verdict:

> God, I am broken. I am undone. I am lost in my grief. Have mercy on my son. Be close to him. Bless him today. Prepare him for the days ahead. New struggles. New opportunities. Father, give me wisdom with Carol. Help me to know how to love her.

MAKING HARD CHOICES

Gene and I realized we had to make a choice every day. Would we give in to despair and depression, or would we go on living a productive life, serving Christ? Would we quit ministry or would we continue to declare that God is good and He is trustworthy?

With so much time passing between Jason's arrest and trial, we already had come to believe that a big part of the Enemy's plan was to destroy our son's future—to ruin his marriage, his career, and his spiritual influence on others. Another part of his plan was to destroy the ministry that Gene and I have in training Christians to communicate their faith effectively through the Speak Up With Confidence seminars and to immobilize me so I couldn't speak at conferences and retreats or have the energy or desire to write books on biblical principles. Less than two years prior to Jason's arrest, Gene and I had launched Speak Up Speaker Services, and we were helping to place over 135 Christian speakers all over the country through the speakers' bureau. People were coming to Christ and God was blessing this new venture in a phenomenal way.

I got even more furious with the Enemy than I had during the hours when I first learned of my son's arrest. When Gene and I once again recognized who our real enemy was, we were suddenly infused with fresh energy and a renewed sense of purpose. We started reading books by other Christians who had gone through the fire and survived. Jim Cymbala's words inspired us: "I discovered an astonishing truth: God is attracted to weakness. He can't resist those who humbly and honestly admit how desperately they need him."[2]

Gene and I resumed our "prayer walking" along the St. Clair River where, almost three years before, I had said to my husband, "Does life get any better than this?" Now we prayed vigorously, with our eyes wide open: "Lord, we are *desperate* for You! This thing that has happened is too big for us to deal with. We are so sad, so disappointed, and so hurt that You didn't rescue our son. We are mad — but we are no longer mad at You. We are *furious* with Satan! He will *not* destroy us! He cannot destroy our son! Regardless of what he has done, J.P. belongs to *You*."

We prayed that God would surround J.P. with angels and protect him from attack — physically and spiritually. My heart agonized over the potential physical threats he was about to encounter in a maximum-security prison environment. We asked God to give him purpose and meaning and to help him to see at least one opportunity daily where he could join God wherever He was at work on the prison compound. We asked for protection, comfort, and encouragement for April, Chelsea, and Hannah, and that God would give Jason and April creative vehicles for keeping their marriage alive in the midst of unthinkable circumstances. We prayed that God would not allow us to waste this great sorrow and that He would reveal specific ways that we could speak up for those who could not speak up for themselves. Foremost on our minds were the families of prisoners — an almost forgotten part of our society.

Gene and I claimed 2 Corinthians 4:16-18 (MSG) as our mantra:

> So we're not giving up. How could we! Even though on the outside
> it often looks like things are falling apart on us, on the inside, where
> God is making new life, not a day goes by without his unfolding grace.
> These hard times are small potatoes compared to the coming good

times, the lavish celebration prepared for us. There's far more here than meets the eye. The things we see now are here today, gone tomorrow. But the things we can't see now will last forever.

Without purpose, a person begins to die a slow death. Our confusion about finding purpose in life comes when we perceive that meaning is only experienced when we reach a predetermined goal or a sought-after resolution to a challenging problem. But Oswald Chambers reframes the concept of purpose this way:

> What is my vision of God's purpose for me? Whatever it may be, His purpose is for me to depend on Him and on His power now. If I can stay calm, faithful, and unconfused while in the middle of the turmoil of life, the goal of the purpose of God is being accomplished in me. God is not working toward a particular finish — His purpose is the process itself. . . . It is the process, not the outcome, that is glorifying to God.[3]

There is a huge piece of my heart that wants my purpose to involve a positive outcome for my son. But I am not the author of the grand story God is writing. During this chapter of life, God's will for Gene and me is that we join Him now in what He wants to accomplish through the process of today's suffering. Our perspective is changing as we realize we are in a spiritual battle here on earth, and we are called to be warriors.

Humanly speaking, we are geared to "do" something, but we are finding that the most empowering way we can do battle is to lay down our weapons of anger and unforgiveness and embrace God's relentless love. This love baffles and confuses the Enemy because it's a love he doesn't understand. Instead of running from God in the middle of our suffering, we are running to God. When this choice is lived out, a heart sacrifice can become a megaphone proclaiming hope, joy, meaning, and passion to those watching in the gallery of life.

MORE *to the* STORY

During the Middle Ages and even in the Modern Age, life was often perceived as a story with a beginning, a middle, and an ending. Life had a plot and there were key characters. People envisioned themselves as playing a part in a much larger story than their own.

Many people living in our postmodern world have a different worldview. People play a role in their own small story and have no vision for what is happening to them as being a part of God's grand story.

Abraham knew he was living in God's grand story. As he traveled from Beersheba to Mt. Moriah, his vision was not just on the sacrifice he had been asked to make. His sight was on the bigger picture of pleasing the God who loved him more than he loved his Isaac. Abraham knew there was more to the story, because he believed God's earlier promise.

The story of Abraham and Isaac is a foreshadowing of what God intended to do through Christ. From before time, the Triune God has been the kind of Being who sacrifices what He holds most dear. The Father sacrifices His own Son, the Son willingly sacrifices His own life — for a good and holy purpose. The Triune God has always been essentially giving, willing to take on pain when He could have avoided it, seeking the good of the creatures He made. The God who asks us to sacrifice is the One who has gone through it Himself. He's not off somewhere in heaven demanding that we suffer while He sits comfortably aloof on the sidelines and observes.

Jesus kept saying over and over to His disciples,

> "If any of you wants to serve me, then follow me. Then you'll be where I am, ready to serve at a moment's notice. The Father will honor and reward anyone who serves me. Right now I am storm-tossed. And what am I going to say? 'Father, get me out of this'? No, this is why I came in the first place. I'll say, 'Father, put your glory on display.'"[4]

Abraham passed this sense of destiny on to Isaac. Isaac passed his faith on to both his sons — Jacob and Esau. One of them wrestled with God face-to-face,

man-to-man, heart-to-heart. That son was Jacob. Leslie Williams describes this
night wrestling:

> When I picture Jacob wrestling all night with God, I see the two of
> them ... thrashing around alone in the middle of the desert, kick-
> ing up tufts of sand underneath a black, star-speckled sky. Jacob's
> sweaty body glistens, muscles taut with determination. He breathes
> heavily and seems exhausted. In spite of his thigh wound, he refuses
> to let go of his opponent until he receives a blessing. In the morning
> ... Jacob is rewarded:
>
> He has seen God face to face. Though he limps, the glimpse of
> the Almighty has changed his identity forever.[5]

As Gene and I have continued to relinquish our control over the outcome of our son's life, we have simultaneously found ourselves speaking
up with confident expectation, begging God to bring blessing out of such
unspeakable circumstances. We continue to wrestle with the God who loves
us with purity, passion, and intensity. He sees our tears, mingled with our
desperation. But inextricably entwined with our humanness is our inner
"knowing" that God is so trustworthy that He will accomplish His purposes, even in this ... this thing that is so mind-boggling, so destructive, so
erosive, so full of pain and suffering. With Jacob, we declare to God, "I will
not let you go unless you bless me."[6] As a result, we, too, walk with a limp.
You can't see it because it's internal. It's a battle scar we carry because we
are warriors of Christ in a fallen world where unthinkable things happen
every day.

I am learning that I can focus the deep passions of my heart on the injustices in the world, on the pain and unfairness of life, on my fears for my son, on
my disappointments and unfulfilled expectations — or I can view my situation
as a piece of a much bigger production that I am not scripting. I have the awe-
some privilege of playing a role in God's grand story, in a drama that does not
waste sorrow. This story has a positive ending.

TOUCHING OUR SON . . . FINALLY

Our first opportunity to have a contact visit with our son following his arrest was, ironically, on Independence Day 2002. After two-and-a-half years of visits to the county jail, I would enter a prison for the first time in my entire life — to see my only child. When Gene and I arrived at the Avon Park facility, forty-five minutes south of Orlando, we had to be fingerprinted and then our identification pictures were taken. My tears wouldn't stop, so I have one of the saddest mug shots imaginable. I wondered if I would be visiting my son in this way for the rest of my life.

We were allowed through a gate that buzzed after we were fully processed, and then we moved into a building where we were searched for contraband and/ or illegal substances. I had to pull the bottom of my bra away from my chest and prove that nothing was hidden inside. We were told to remove our shoes and show the guard the bottoms of our feet. After that we were patted down, and finally we were allowed into the visitation area. Gene and I then stood near the door inside the visitation room where we knew our son would be coming through momentarily.

I was filled with emotion. J.P. walked through the door and flashed us a big smile. Then he walked over to the check-in table to declare the kind of shoes, watch, and wedding ring he was wearing to the corrections officer. At long last, he was allowed to turn and greet us.

My son put his arms around me, placed his cheek on my cheek, hugged me, kissed me, and hugged some more, while allowing my tears to soak the front of his prison uniform. J.P. turned to hug his father, and I could see that Gene was overwhelmed with emotion as well. During our visit, we were allowed to hold our son's hands, touch his arm, and sit next to him at a table. I know how important touch is in conveying love, and my son had been without meaningful touch for over two years and nine months.

While enjoying this long-forbidden privilege, my heart was dealing with the agony of realizing that even though the visitation conditions were much improved in the prison over what they had been in the county jail, this was all we were going to get for the rest of our lives — apart from a miracle that would allow our son to once again walk in freedom. The finality of that thought made me shudder.

NEW KINDS *of* "NORMAL"

Sometimes "laying our Isaac down" involves acknowledging that life will never be the same as it once was.

Jill wrote to me:

> I have four small children, ages six and under. Sarah, one of my twins, has severe challenges. After months of waiting to see a specialist at the University of Michigan, we were given the news just two weeks before her third birthday, "Your daughter has moderate to severe autism. Sarah doesn't speak, gives us almost no eye contact, and she has social problems. The life I envisioned for my twin girls is vanishing before my eyes.
>
> This has been a hard hit. I truly believe David and I are still functioning because of the support and prayers of family and my church. I keep thinking of a line you said at the conference you did for our women last fall. You said, "Even in this . . . " I cannot tell you how often I have cried out to God and said, "Yes, Lord, even in this . . . I trust You. I love You. I will obey You. I will honor You." I know the Lord Jesus can do anything. We are making the necessary plans to care for Sarah in the best possible way, but we're also holding on to the hope that she will get better. For now, we are adjusting to a new kind of "normal."

Adjusting to "a new kind of normal" is an important part of a heart sacrifice for many of us. Gene and I are realizing that part of our new "normal" is that instead of flying to an exotic port somewhere in the world to see our son, the U.S. naval officer, we plan vacations to Florida, where we spend our weekends waiting in the prison visitation line. Visitation times are on Saturdays and

Sundays from 9:00 A.M. to 3:00 P.M. That doesn't mean we get in at 9:00 A.M., but we can begin standing in the visitation line at that time. If the fingerprinting equipment is working correctly, we might see our child within thirty to forty minutes — if the line is short. If screening equipment is malfunctioning, it might take an hour and a half to get in. By 2:45 P.M., all visitors must begin standing in the exit lines.

We have been surprised to discover that in the midst of this "adjusted life plan" we are slowly experiencing an unexpected sense of purpose. Instead of planning all of our leisure time around self-indulgent activities, our minds are keenly aware of the needs of the people around us. As we meet other families in the visitation area at the men's correctional facility, we pray for them and talk to their children and engage them in playful bantering. When appropriate, we ask the parents how long they have been coming to visit their son and how they are holding up in the midst of such difficult circumstances. We've discovered that "vending café" food at the picnic tables in the prison yard can be made into an extraordinary feast when you are spending time with the people you love. We spend more time talking to each other and playing games as a family because those are things we *can* do, and these activities bring us closer together. Our "new normal" certainly isn't what we would have chosen; but it's what we have to work with, so we embrace it.

A new thought was beginning to take root within us during the hours we spent standing in line to go through security with people we might never have met under "normal" circumstances. There was sadness, brokenness, hurt, and pain on all sides. The family members of the inmates had their own grief-riddled stories of what had happened to bring them to this visitation line. *Perhaps,* Gene and I thought, *God was allowing us to get a glimpse of another side of life because we had the network and resources to provide a ray of hope to do something to help.*

Each visitation day brings new opportunities. We meet some people who are withdrawn, due to the pain, lack of trust, and wounds of the past, and we respect their need for privacy. Others are angry at being thrust into a situation they didn't create and have no power to change. Sometimes when I see the tears or anger in another mother in the visitation line, I make brief eye contact and say, "I know. It hurts a lot." Sometimes it opens a door to talk. Sometimes not. I understand.

When we became the parents of an inmate, we heard the cries of the poor, in particular. "The fifteen-minute collect calls we get from our son cost us over six dollars each." Gene and I were stunned to find out that local calls were so expensive. After we got our own bill from MCI, the approved company for connecting the prison telephones with our telephone line via collect calls, we discovered that one fifteen-minute long-distance call from Florida to Michigan was almost twenty-two dollars. We realized that families were being torn apart by the inability to afford communicating with each other regularly. The families of inmates were being overcharged for telephone calls, and nobody seemed to know who made the money off these calls or who could do anything about it. With national long distance rates as low as three to five cents a minute, why was the prison system gouging the families of prisoners who were already in difficult financial straits?

One day Gene called the telephone company to try to get to the bottom of the *why* question regarding the exorbitant telephone charges. After being put on hold multiple times, the MCI employee, desperately trying to come up with a reason, said, "Well, I think it's part of the punishment for what the guys did to get into prison."

Once Gene and I got beyond our anger about the unfairness within the prison system regarding the exorbitant telephone charges, the lack of response to returning our calls about visitation guidelines, the total absence of family friendly visitation areas for inmates with young children, and the aggravation of not having soap or towels for our hands in the restrooms in the visitation area, we moved into a different mental and spiritual mode. Our thoughts started to get creative. One day I penned in my journal:

> Lord, I've been complaining so much about everything that's wrong
> with the Department of Corrections that I totally forgot to thank
> You for the corrections officer who treated me with respect and
> kindness when she took me through the security procedure last week.

Thank You for the other CO who brought in new coloring books and crayons for Chelsea and Hannah and for the other young children during our last visit. Thank You for the smile I got from the girlfriend of one of the inmates I met last month in the visitation line. Thank You that J.P. was allowed to order tennis shoes through "the system" that will enable him to enjoy his love of running and staying physically fit with much greater comfort.

As I started listing small but steady blessings, I began thinking beyond my frustrations. Jason was inside a maximum-security prison; Gene and I were outside. We had the opportunity to research what specific resources could help the inmates to become educated, mentored, and encouraged, and to begin the process of rehabilitation and restoration because Jason and April were experiencing firsthand what the greatest needs were. Gene and I were regularly meeting the families of prisoners and beginning to understand the major challenges they faced—financially, personally, and spiritually. We started taking mental notes every time we communicated with officers at the prison, or interacted with the families of inmates, or talked to one of the chaplains. We began asking ourselves, *What can we DO to educate, encourage, support positive change, and improve the climate for the inmates and for their families in a way that could produce hope, faith, and a positive future?*

We had been training people in communication skills from a Christian perspective through Speak Up With Confidence seminars for many years. At the beginning of the launch of that ministry, I sensed God's urging to remember that part of my responsibility was to speak up for people who could not speak up for themselves. I didn't know at the time, of course, that God would burden me so heavily with the need to speak up for the needs of the families of incarcerated individuals. But now He was giving me a deeply personal conviction to follow King Lemuel's admonitions in the Old Testament: "Speak up for the people who have no voice, for the rights of all the down-and-outers. Speak out for justice! Stand up for the poor and destitute!"[7]

We brainstormed with family members and friends, many of whom had been our Stretcher Bearers during the worst of our family crisis. Our emerging vision to help "the least of these" was met with tremendous enthusiasm. We didn't want to duplicate what Prison Fellowship was already doing so successfully in taking the gospel to inmates and ministering to prisoners' children, but we also knew that our sphere of influence would reach a different group of people who could offer support and help to a desperately needy part of our society.

Once again I opened my journal and recorded a few of the ways individuals and churches had supported us in meaningful ways. During the weekend when I spoke for the women's retreat for Grace Chapel in Lexington, Massachusetts, I shared with the women's ministries director that the prison chapel where Jason was located had just eliminated the use of transparencies for the worship songs that were sung in the chapel services because the funds for running the chapel were not sufficient to pay the licensing fee for legal use of the lyrics. The women of Grace immediately decided to make it their ministry to pay the licensing fee.

After hearing about our family crisis, the women of Mountain Christian Church in Joppa, Maryland, contacted us to ask if they could "adopt" our Florida family and begin meeting some of their tangible needs. They provided birthday gifts, encouraging notes, and a check that April could use toward the telephone charges that made family communication with J.P. possible. Their support was such an encouragement, I wondered what could happen if churches all over the country adopted a prison family in their own geographical area.

Many more ideas continued to emerge, mostly because of the creative ways the Stretcher Bearers had already ministered to us. How could we help others the way we had been helped? God was transforming my root of bitterness over all of the bad things that had happened into a sturdy tree of faith, hope, and positive action. I began to believe that God could indeed give "beauty for ashes, the oil of joy for mourning, the garment of praise for the spirit of heaviness"[8]—and that He could be glorified even in this heinous and painful experience of the past four years.

There are days in your life when you pray and feel no response, get no answer, and have no hope. I had experienced many days when it felt like God wasn't answering my prayers. In fact, it felt like God was saying, "No." I had almost forgotten my underlying prayer throughout this ordeal: "Lord, please don't allow us to waste our sorrow. Turn this evil and hurtful event into something that will give You glory and further Your kingdom work. Help us to fit in with Your purposes. We know You didn't plan what happened, but help us to turn what the Enemy intended for our destruction into a joyful celebration of Your power and greatness." Together Gene and I prayed, "We are available to do what You want us to do."

In early 2004 we launched a nonprofit organization, Speak Up for Hope. We pray that God will use this endeavor to give hope to the hopeless, encouragement and strength to the weary, reparation to marriages that have been torn apart by incarceration, and mental, spiritual, and physical stability to the children of prisoners. We pray that people all over the world will begin speaking up for those who cannot speak up for themselves. As people become the hands and feet of Jesus to "the least of these," something miraculous happens. They are personally transformed from the inside out, and they model for others how to be a Stretcher Bearer, a rope holder, a hope giver.

STEPPING-STONES *to a* NEW REALITY

Heart sacrifices are empowering choices when we understand that we have made the right decision. They are never easy choices because they deal with the most personal and vulnerable places in our lives, but they become the stepping-stones to renewed confidence and positive action, and to a platform for speaking up about an authentic relationship with the God who loved us enough to lay down the life of His son.

Something I'm speaking up about is my conviction that God's design for the future of my son is for his good and for God's glory. However, as much as I spiritually and intellectually understand that concept, and as much as I believe God is more interested in the process of our struggle than in the particulars connected with reaching a desired goal, there are days when I still cope poorly.

Eleven months and three weeks following Jason's verdict and sentencing, we received a phone call from attorney Barbara Davis informing us that our son's request for an appeal had been refused by the appellate court. The devastating news came just days before Easter weekend, and we had already made plans to go to Florida for April's birthday and to see J.P. on Easter Sunday. I sat in the Orlando airport and wrote:

> April 19, 2003 — Today is the one-year anniversary of one of the darkest days of my life — my son's conviction for first-degree murder and his sentencing — life without parole. Gene and I flew to Florida on separate planes because cheap seats were limited when we purchased our tickets. I think God gave me the gift of aloneness on this day — freedom to feel my grief, time to think, time to hurt, without the interruption of conversation. I like to be sad alone.
>
> My plane landed an hour and a half ahead of Gene's. As I boarded the tram that took me to the baggage claim area, I was met with the usual myriad of young families who are in Orlando for their first trip to Disney World. The tram was buzzing with exaggerated animation and with the joy of children who are headed for celebration. The digitized voice on the speakers heralded a welcome to those coming "for business travel, for a return trip home, and for the visitors who are coming to one of Orlando's world-class attractions." An invisible arrow pierced my heart and I found myself sarcastically adding, "and a very special welcome to the parents of our Florida State prisoners! Enjoy your stay and come back soon."
>
> Sarcasm is a curious thing. When fed, it grows and becomes a hovering vulture in the mind. It's like the weather — sometimes hanging over me like a heavy cloud on a gray Michigan morning. One of the lessons of this journey is that I have to fight sarcasm and cynicism by filling my mind with things that are excellent and praiseworthy.

I decided to write out my prayer for the weekend ahead:

God, tomorrow is Easter Sunday, and instead of going to church singing victorious songs about Your resurrection, I will be entering a maximum-security state penitentiary, and I will visit my son inside the razor wire. My heart is breaking and I long to bring my only child hope, encouragement, comfort, and a promise of future, but I have nothing to give. If I allow myself to hope that I will one day see my son walk in freedom again, am I setting myself up for more disappointment and pain? Give us the grace we need to encourage J.P. and April after receiving such devastating news about the possibility of an appeal. Help all of us to hold on to hope. Amen.

As I finished the prayer, Gene appeared on the escalator and we made our way to our family. We left the house early the next morning and drove to the facility. On Easter Sunday we sat at a picnic table and read the story of Jesus' arrest, His scourging, His death by crucifixion, and His resurrection. We proclaimed as a family of faith: "He is risen! He is risen INDEED!" We sat in our razor-wire sanctuary and sang "Christ Arose."

At that moment I knew we were experiencing the power of the resurrection because we had supernatural joy, peace, and purpose. The Enemy tried to destroy our hope, but he failed again on Easter morning. We felt empowered to join the ranks of others who are engaged in the great adventure of being Christ-followers, even when it's hard. That day we stomped on the head of the Enemy! It felt good. We were beginning to experience the truth of God's words to Isaiah: "I will give you treasures hidden in the darkness — secret riches. I will do this so you may know that I am the LORD, the God of Israel, the one who calls you by name."[9]

Our lives won't ever be the same. And on my good days, that's okay. We are privileged to carry His banner and demonstrate to the world that they can make it too. So much more is ahead. We are waiting, with hope. Gary Thomas puts it this way: "Waiting, for the believer, is not the futile and desperate act of those who have no other options, but rather a confident trust that eventually God will set things right."[10]

THE POWER *of* SPEAKING UP

A heart sacrifice is a positive choice, not a defensive reaction. God gives us the incredible opportunity to join Him on a journey of discovery — where we find meaning in chaos, purpose in pain, the cup of joy in the cup of sorrow, hope in the midst of grief, and purpose and empowerment in telling our stories.

What's in a story? The opportunity to give hope to somebody else. Rick Warren says,

> Personal stories are . . . easier to relate to than principles, and people love to hear them. They capture our attention, and we remember them longer. . . . Shared stories build a relational bridge that Jesus can walk across from your heart to theirs.[11]

There is a common ground of understanding, forgiveness, acceptance, and healing when we are authentic with each other. When we tell our real-life stories of what we have encountered on the journey of life, we break down barriers and create safe places to risk revealing the truth. Intimacy in our relationships springs to life when we are no longer hiding behind the mask of denial, embarrassment, guilt, or shame. We're just us — people who have had some good days in life and people who have had some very bad days. We've quit pretending that everything is "fine" and that life is grand. When we share our stories with each other, we find a way of relating without the façade and without the need to impress. We can just be real. This brings tremendous freedom.

Frederick Buechner writes, "My assumption is that the story of any one of us is in some measure the story of all of us."[12] I have found this to be true. Sharing our stories helps us to quickly get out of the self-defeating pattern of trying to figure out who is suffering more. We are all suffering to one degree or another. Is the woman whose husband betrayed her by having an affair with her best friend hurting more than I am? Is the man who is choosing to keep his marriage vows to a woman who is too self-centered to consider his feelings and needs in less emotional pain than I am? Is the man who was an award-winning athlete who broke his back and is now a quadriplegic worse off than my son? Is the couple who lost their home and had to declare bankruptcy due to corporate downsizing in worse straits than I am? Do the men and women tackling their deepest internal wounds and practicing rigorous recovery programs in order to lay down devastating addictions have it easier than I do? Is the woman who just gave birth to a child with Down's Syndrome in more anguish than I am? Are the parents who poured their love, resources, and encouragement into their child who is strung out on drugs in my level of pain?

The bottom line is that it doesn't matter. We are all a bunch of flawed human beings living in an imperfect world. When we start sharing our Isaac experiences with each other, we build trust, faith, and hope. We don't need a meter to tell us which pain hurts the most. All of our heartaches produce great sadness, and telling our stories to each other brings a release, a comfort, and the knowledge that somebody cares.

I met inspirational speaker Jackie Kendall in Indiana where we were sharing the platform at the Winsome Women Retreat. Her vibrant, effusive love for Jesus permeated the heart of everyone in the audience — including mine. At the end of Jackie's first message, she called me up to the platform and presented me with a gift — an exquisite bracelet, with tiny silver squares, spelling out the name, *Ephraim.* Jackie explained:

Carol, we have not met before, but I have been told of your suffering, and I had a jeweler make this gift for you. In Genesis, Joseph (son of Jacob, grandson of Isaac, great-grandson of Abraham) is naming one of his sons: "The second son he named Ephraim and said, 'It is because God has made me fruitful in the land of my suffering.'"[13] In Hebrew, Ephraim means "double fruit." The Lord used the name Ephraim as a reminder that a person can be fruitful in suffering.

In Genesis 48 Joseph brings his two sons, Manasseh and Ephraim, to his father, Jacob, so he can bless them before he dies. Joseph carefully positions his sons beside Jacob so that the firstborn, Manasseh, will be blessed above the second-born son, Ephraim. But something surprising happens: Jacob crossed his arms and deliberately puts his right hand on the younger boy's head. Why would Jacob go against tradition and bless Ephraim above Manasseh? The blessing was: "May God make you like EPHRAIM and Manasseh."

Why would "fruitful in suffering" be the lead blessing and not Manassah, which means, "It is because God has made me forget all my trouble and all my father's household"?[14]

Maybe it's because getting over a painful past is a wonderful accomplishment, but producing fruit through a painful past is a miraculous event. Being fruitful in suffering, being an "Ephraim," brings glory to God — who alone can give the grace-filled capacity to face the unthinkable and be fruitful in the unimaginable.

That day Jackie blessed me with much more than a lovely piece of jewelry. She challenged me to embrace the Ephraim blessing. As I daily lay my Isaac down, I don't just want to be known as a woman who has made the heart sacrifice of relinquishing my will for my only child. I am asking God to allow me the privilege of being *fruitful* in suffering.

Sometimes I look back on the past four years and ask: How is God reshaping my life and ministry? How is He changing me? How are my responses to people different than before our crisis? Is there really a "privilege" connected to this nightmare of an experience?

As much as I have hated the process, I know that I am more in love with Jesus than before. I know He loves me more than I love my "Isaac." Instead of giving advice to people who are in difficult circumstances, I listen. I cry more often — not just for myself and for my son, but for the deep needs of others.

Perhaps the biggest change is in my prayer life. I used to think of prayer as a specific thing I did when I sat down to "do devotions" with my Bible in hand and no interruptions in sight. Everything about the way I pray is different now. I pray with my eyes wide open all the time. I'm growing in understanding the whole "pray without ceasing" concept because I'm so needy that I have eyes to see the needs of the people around me. When I walk into a room, I pray for the people I see. During conversations with others, I'm praying for them, their families, their needs, and their hurts.

As I walk in the visitation area at the prison, I pray for the families seated around tables and for the children who are playing nearby. I pray that my son will find meaning and hope in every day and that he will know his life still has a purpose. I cover my grandchildren, Chelsea and Hannah, with prayer, asking God to make His presence palpable in their lives, to comfort and heal them in the deepest parts of their souls. I pray that God will bless J.P. and April's marriage and that they will continue to find creative ways to express their love to one another, even though they have no opportunity for physical intimacy.

My view of this world and the world to come is different. I am aware of the brevity of life and of the need to use my sphere of influence to help others. I know that there can be fruitfulness in suffering because I am experiencing it. Not the kind of fruitfulness I once knew — one that was measured by achievements and productivity, but a deeper, richer, more meaningful fruitfulness that is based on a love relationship with Jesus. A relationship that begins with loving Him more and letting that love spill into the lives of others. This focus takes the "work" out of my Christianity because I don't have to perform. I just get to "be" His child, and He is my Daddy. He loves me whether or not I disappoint Him. He teaches me priceless lessons on choosing hope over despair. He opens His arms and lets me crawl into His comfortable embrace. And I am safe.

God's Power in *Your* Circumstances

I used to wonder how any good could come out of reviewing the details and reliving the pain of an unwanted experience. But I've discovered that tremendous power is released when we dare to speak up and communicate our personal stories with honesty and vulnerability. By doing so we remind others that life is an unpredictable journey for all of us. Bad things happen, and the Enemy tries to destroy our spirit and our sense of purpose. If we can remember that we are engaged in a spiritual battle — not with weapons and hatred, but with hope, faith, and joy — we affirm our ultimate security in God and our love for Him in the midst of our heartache. The grace-filled reward is that we find ourselves enveloped in steadfast, intimate, extravagant love that continues to move us into the heart of the greatest adventure of all.

"God is keeping careful watch over us and the future. The Day is coming when you'll have it all — life healed and whole . . . Pure gold put in the fire comes out of it *proved* pure; genuine faith put through this suffering comes out *proved* genuine. When Jesus wraps this all up, it's your faith, not your gold, that God will have on display as evidence of his victory. You never saw him, yet you love him. You still don't see him, yet you trust him — with laughter and singing. Because you kept on believing, you'll get what you're looking forward to: total salvation."[15]

1. In what specific ways can you begin to act on the fact that in God's grand story, "we win"? Begin a list of the victories — small and large — that you can envision or are already experiencing as you live through your Isaac experience. (Consider that finding the strength and sense of purpose to do even basic life tasks, like continuing to get out of bed in the morning, is a significant victory in light of the devastation the Enemy was bound to accomplish.)

2. On page 163 I wrote: "Instead of running from God in the middle of our suffering, we are running to God." On a scale from 0 to 10, how true is this for you right now? How might praying, as I did, that God will not allow you to "waste your sorrow" give you needed faith, hope, and joy?

3. Like Gene and me, everyone who is living with the heartache and loss of an Isaac experience must make a choice every day — a choice between paralyzing despair and energizing faith. What specific choices do you need to make today and in the week ahead that will enable you to go on living a productive life and serving Christ with a "warrior" mentality? Talk to God about these choices, and ask Him to give you supernatural "resurrection" power, one day at a time.

4. In what ways have you needed to adjust to "a new kind of normal" as a result of your heart sacrifice? Journal or write a letter to God about the specifics and how you feel. If you or others have new and

different needs because of this revised "normal," boldly ask Him to meet those needs in creative ways that only He could think up!

5. Start a "blessings" list. For at least five minutes, refuse to think about your sorrow and frustration, and focus instead on the positive things you see in the midst of your Isaac experience. No matter how small the blessing — like the smile I received from someone in the prison visitation line — write it down and offer a prayer of gratitude to God.

6. Consider a time when you have been on the giving or receiving end of the power of a shared story. Record some of the benefits of this experience, and ask God to use your current story as a "bridge that Jesus can walk over" from your heart to someone else's.

THE *M*ELODY OF THE FUTURE

THE HOLIDAYS WERE APPROACHING AND I WAS DREADING this fifth Christmas season we were facing without our son's presence filling the house with his characteristic enthusiasm and energy.

I gazed out the window facing the St. Clair River. Everything about the scene reminded me that we were entering a new season. The hearty fuchsia geraniums and decorative asparagus fern on the patio had lasted into mid-November, but now the flowerpots were ice-covered shadows of their former beauty. No cars were visible on the parkway along the river. The skateboarders and bicyclers had disappeared, and everything within my immediate sight was a reminder that fall was over, trees were barren, snow was falling, and the long, freezing winter lay ahead of us.

This melancholy mood led me to the lower level of the house to the spare bedroom closet. Early in our journey, large boxes of Jason's Naval Academy uniforms, personal items, and handwritten journals had been shipped to our home. With great compassion and kindness, my administrative assistant, Shirley, emptied several of the boxes and hung up my son's clothing, knowing the job of going through those boxes would be too much for my heart to endure. The door had been closed on that closet for a long time.

Opening the door on my private pain, my eyes immediately gravitated to J.P.'s dress whites — the same uniform he was married in. I slowly ran my hands over the collar, the sleeves, the buttons, and the medals. As I lovingly touched item after item of my son's clothing, I came to a dress shirt that had obviously been worn once without being laundered. I noticed the soiled neck ring on the collar. (Moms notice things like that.) I held the shirt in my arms for a long time, sniffing the collar, in search of the scent of days gone by — a happier, peaceful, prideful, and easier time in my life. I glanced at a box of J.P.'s favorite books. Oh, how he loved books! Fresh tears cascaded down my cheeks as I fingered and refolded his old T-shirts and running shorts. Everything had changed. Nothing would ever be the same. I tried on his hiking boots and wept some more.

With heavy hearts, Gene and I put up the Christmas tree and hung boughs and bows on the open staircase. We were hosting a Michigan family reunion and then leaving for Florida to spend a week with J.P., April, and the girls. My sister Paula was flying to Tampa to join us. J.P. had been moved to the maximum-security Hardee Correctional Institution just six months before, after a year-long stay at Avon Park.

After going through security at Hardee, we saw that J.P. looked good as he emerged from the security checkpoint. His "prison blues" looked like well-pressed hospital scrubs and matched his distinctive clear blue eyes perfectly. His joy in seeing us was obvious. "Auntie Foo Foo" (our descriptive nickname for my fabulously flamboyant sister) brought love, warmth, humor, and joy to our visit. I sat back and listened as the two of them talked honestly about the wily ways of depression and of how both of them are learning to combat this slippery, life-destroying enemy of the soul.

We talked together nonstop for five hours, catching up on J.P.'s work as one of the assistants to the prison chaplain and brainstorming about how to best serve others through Speak Up for Hope, the new nonprofit organization Gene and I were about to launch. I could see fresh purpose and passion on J.P.'s face as he recounted the needs of the inmates and their families, anticipating that our new organization could provide a ray of hope for some of the most needy people in our society.

We were allowed a total of three visits with J.P. during this holiday trip, and on the day of our final visit I stepped into the ladies' room. While seated in one of the stalls, I heard a woman walk in. She was sobbing, and her words spilled out in a torrent of anguish: "I hate this place! I hate these G-damn people! I can't breathe. I think I'm having a nervous breakdown." As I opened the door of my stall to offer help and comfort, I realized she just needed somebody to hear her pain. Even before I saw her face, I was already weeping because my heart identified so intensely with her anguish. I listened more than I talked. It was her first visit to the Hardee facility. I nodded with understanding and many more fresh tears of my own as she voiced her total frustration with the prison system. She seemed comforted. Someone had heard her desperation.

Later, I journaled my reflections on this fifth Christmas season behind the razor wire:

> Life is very different than it was before. It's harder. More challenging. Agonizingly painful. But different in a good way too.
>
> I've discovered the joy of simplicity. Jason's life is uncomplicated without the accumulation of "stuff," the pressures of career advancement, the exhausting drive to achieve status and to impress people.
>
> I've learned that tears create a common ground with all classes of people. Pain is pain is pain is pain. Mothers who are hurting do not feel envious, spiteful, or resentful of other mothers who are hurting. Our shared heartache produces an instant connection not based on status, achievement, or income level.
>
> I'm trying to be a gracious receiver, and I'm learning how to be an extravagant giver. Our Stretcher Bearers have modeled what it means to "be Jesus" to us, and in doing so, they have forever changed our lives. I can no longer walk over to the other side of the road when someone in my path needs help.

I thought back to the days just prior to the event that turned our world upside-down, when I looked up at my husband and asked, "Does life get any better than *this*?" I asked myself if I could honestly say we are entering a new season of purpose in this journey. The gut-level truth is that there are still numerous days when I hate my life. But last weekend during those few minutes with the desperate woman in the ladies' room, I had the privilege of being the hands and feet of Jesus to her. As she cussed, wept, and hyperventilated,

God allowed me to buffer her pain. I didn't preach to her. I didn't give advice. I didn't quote Bible verses on suffering. I simply cried with her. I don't even know her name. We were both weeping so hard we couldn't speak. But she knew someone cared. It felt good to love her unconditionally in the same way Jesus has been loving me.

The strange paradox is that in the middle of Jason's hopeless sentence of life without the possibility of parole, Gene and I are living out our own life sentence of dashed hopes. But with dashed hopes comes the possibility of new dreams. Dreams that are forged by fire, heartache, and suffering are made of strong metals, and we see more opportunities all the time that make us feel privileged to be walking this path of heart sacrifice. Richard Alves summarized our thoughts when he said, "Hope is hearing the melody of the future. Faith is to dance to it now."[1]

In a brand-new way I was also beginning to envision J.P.'s purpose for this season of his life. As he meets men every day in the middle of a prison routine that has very little variety, he can choose to hear the melody of the future as he invests his time in encouraging those who have no hope, or he can give in to despair or depression. He can practice the discipline of unshakable faith as he dances in step to a melody that is currently out of earshot, or he can close his ears to the possibility of ever hearing the music. It's a choice all of us have to make (sometimes daily) in the middle of our Isaac experiences.

As always, the hardest part of our holiday visit was the final goodbye. We hugged tightly, as long as the guards would allow. Jason stood in the line along the back wall to be searched before reentering the main prison compound. We stood in the line with other visitors to exit the razor wire. Our lingering glances and waves produced a conflicted mixture of sadness and joy.

Gene and I returned home on the weekend following New Year's Day, and later that week I once again pulled out my journal and wrote as I gazed out the window facing the river:

The weatherman said we'll be getting up to five more inches of
snow by tomorrow. On some days it seems that spring will never

come, and today I feel caught up in a never-ending winter. But I will get up tomorrow, and I will be one day closer to a positive resolution for my son.

Whether in this lifetime or in the next, Jason will one day walk in freedom. Until that day arrives in all of its splendor and glory, I will never quit praying for a miracle of mercy and grace for my only child. I will also never cease to pray for the Miller family, and I will always hurt for the great losses of everyone who has been negatively impacted by my son's actions.

I put my pen down and realized afresh how drastically God had adjusted our life-plan. Glancing through some notes I made much earlier in this journey, I came to Jim Cymbala's tender observation: "God does His most stunning work where things seem hopeless and wherever there is pain, suffering, and desperation, Jesus is."[2]

In the middle of our circumstances, which do not appear to be changing, we are finding a resurgence of hope and a renewed faith. Gene and I are engaging ourselves in the ongoing adventure of a lifetime — trusting God, without knowing where it will lead us or how it will fit into God's grand story. When I am the most desperate, my Abba Father opens His arms, holds me tenderly, and I am comforted. I know I am loved. And I don't have to know the end of the story, because He does.

If Gene and I had never endured unthinkable circumstances, we might not have understood the pain of brokenness. If we had gotten our miracle easily and quickly, we wouldn't have experienced the needs of "the least of these" in our society. If there had been "a lamb in the thicket" for our family, we wouldn't have launched Speak Up for Hope. If life hadn't held unspeakable tragedy, we never would have been the recipients of such extravagant love.

What I am writing today is not the end of this story. It is only the beginning. Many more chapters will be written, as they will for all of us. The surprising discovery is that in letting go of our Isaacs, there is an emerging awareness of God's relentless love. Michael Yaconelli said it well:

(God) loves us when we don't want him to love us. He loves us when we don't act like Christians. He loves us when our lives are a mess. His love is sticky, resistant to rejection, aggressive, and persistent. The challenge is on, so go ahead, resist his love, run from it, hide from it. Go ahead and try.[3]

But you'll lose. So instead, I encourage you to run to Him when you are beaten down, broken into pieces, questioning your faith, and doubting His goodness. If you listen, you will hear Him say the same thing I said to my son on my first visit to the jail: "There is *nothing* that will ever take away my unconditional love for you." Get used to it. God loves people who don't have all the answers.

And if you are still clutching your Isaac to your chest, running around in circles saying, "God's not going to get what I have!" make a choice. Misery or joy? Frenetic activity or relaxation? Control or release? Codependence or God-dependence? Is the alternative to laying down our Isaacs that appealing? I don't think so.

The faith that gets us through unthinkable circumstances begins with being flat-out needy and allowing God's love to wrap us up, hold us close, and dry our tears. One day we discover that our cries are being transformed into life-giving, healthy tears that are rebirthing faith, hope, and joy. And life doesn't get much better than *that*!

❧ ❧ ❧

And now please turn the page for the rest of the story. Sometimes laying your Isaac down is a lifetime process and not just a moment in time.

Ten Years Later . . .
The Power of Perseverance

"One day you'll wake up and discover you can breathe again. This agonizing pain will not be this acute for the rest of your life." My friend was trying to comfort me — to somehow convey that pain has a season when it is so intense you doubt you will be able to go on living. She explained that the mind and body eventually adjust to the reality of a new kind of normal, and life gets more tolerable. She added, "People learn to laugh again, and they become functional, even happy." Her years of counseling, combined with our long friendship, earned her the right to give me this advice. However, at that moment, I didn't want what felt like "false comfort." I just wanted to be alone with my pain.

Now here I am, a full decade after writing *When I Lay My Isaac Down*, and I can admit she was speaking truth to my heart, even though my mind wasn't ready to absorb that thought. Countless people have written to me during the past decade, and their questions are numerous:

- Did Jason get an appeal?
- Are Jason and April still married?
- How old are Chelsea and Hannah now, and do they visit Jason?
- What is your son doing behind the razor wire?
- Has Jason done any writing?
- How often can you visit your son?
- What has happened to your ministry since the murder?
- What do you do through the nonprofit organization Speak Up for Hope?
- Is there any chance Jason will ever walk in freedom?

Many readers have prayed for our family as we live out a story far different from what we anticipated. Thank you for standing in the gap through your powerful intercession.

WHAT DOES PERSEVERANCE *Look* LIKE?

I never understood the meaning of perseverance until I lived "in the meantime," waiting for a better resolution for my son, following the judge's proclamation of his sentence: "Life, without the possibility of parole." Day followed day. Month followed month. Year followed year. Well-meaning people came up to me after speaking engagements and said, "God has told me your son will win his trial."

With emotions rising, I wanted to yell, "Didn't you hear what I said in my message? The trial is over! Jason *did not* win his trial. According to Florida state law, he will be in prison until he dies." But I didn't say it. I only thought it. During the past many years, at several events where I've spoken, people whispered in my ear, "The Lord has revealed to me that your son will be released very soon." At one event, the senior pastor of a large, growing church stood on the platform and proclaimed, "I never say things like this, but God is telling me, '*This* will be the year Jason Kent is released.' Believe with me! Say it out loud with me." Before long the entire congregation began to chant, "This will be the year Jason Kent is released!" The well-known pastor prayed with Gene and me with an authority and confidence that touched me to the soul.

How I wanted to believe it! How I longed for the day when I could take my son home, feed him his favorite meal, and help launch him into a productive, purposeful life outside prison walls. But the year came and went. And Jason is still incarcerated with the same sentence he had on the day his court case ended in April of 2002.

As I grow in my faith, I've learned most people sincerely desire the best for Gene and me and for our son. They long for a positive resolution that would return Jason to a life of freedom, with a chance to redeem past choices and have a fresh start. They care deeply and would never deliberately cause us hurt, so we forgive them quickly, or life would become a permanent disappointment.

We're discovering that the key to making it to each new day is perseverance. The definition of this word is "steadfastness in doing something despite difficulty or delay in achieving success." It is also "continuance in a state of grace leading finally to a state of glory."[1] The past ten years have revealed some important truths:

- Life is short.
- Delayed gratification can make an eventual result more significant.
- God reveals the benefits of "a state of grace that leads to a state of glory" more slowly than I want.

So what does perseverance look like? On the surface, it often looks like nothing is happening. It sometimes feels like a slow death, or like a daily rerun of the movie *Groundhog Day*, where we do the same thing over again every day of the year. I sometimes think it's waiting and wanting a different outcome but not having a "start date" on our anticipated scenario.

But that's not what perseverance is. It's all about a daily choice to live in a state of grace with an eternal perspective. And we've had lots of opportunities to practice!

WHAT CAUSED JASON *to Unravel?*

In the latest book on our journey with Jason, *Between a Rock and a Grace Place*, he shares in his letters what went on in his heart and mind before the murder.

Dear Mom and Dad,

As I write now, almost ten years removed from the horrific day my mind snapped, it is almost impossible to recall exactly what led up to my devastating actions. I remember the intensity of my emotional angst as my ability to protect my beloved stepdaughters appeared to be slipping away. My wife and I had sought legal counsel from a highly recommended lawyer . . . but nothing we did to protect [the girls] from what I believed was an imminent threat to their safety appeared to be working. . . .

I imagined my daughters coming to me in the future, sobbing out the question: "Daddy, couldn't you have done anything to protect us?" In my determination not to abandon my little girls, I was losing my grip on reality and my ability to reason.

As part of the volunteer military, I was willing to stand in harm's way on behalf of my country. . . . While I was still a student at the U.S. Naval Academy, I had to decide if I was willing to lay down my life, if necessary, to protect American citizens. I knew I could. No father would hesitate to sacrifice his life for his children, and I was no different. Now a battle was raging within me between my faith in God and what I felt I had to do to protect my girls. . . .

I know I have caused you so much agony, Mom and Dad, and I can only imagine the pain I have caused the father of the man I killed. I have stolen from him his relationship with his son. . . .

My lack of faith in God led me [to make a devastating choice] that reaped death, devastation, grief, and destruction of everything my life had previously represented.[2]

Because Jason was in the Orlando County Jail for two and a half years before his trial took place, he has now been incarcerated for more than thirteen years. I have watched my son go from a young twenty-five-year-old naval officer to a thirty-eight-year-old man, graying along the temples as I did at his age. I've observed the impetuousness of youth mature into a man who takes full responsibility for the devastation of his actions with remorse and deep grief for the family of the deceased, for the loneliness and pain his actions perpetrated upon his wife and stepdaughters, and for the reverberating sadness and long-term impact felt by his parents.

THE YEARS *Following* THE CONVICTION

Following Jason's trial and sentencing, we went through all the steps involved in appealing at both the state and the federal levels, to no avail. It was a long, expensive, discouraging process. All of us realize a life was taken and there is rightfully a heavy price to be paid, and some would say the only justice is for him to spend the remainder of his life in prison, but how we longed for the hope that Jason would one day walk in freedom.

Then a most unexpected e-mail arrived from an influential person in a government position in Florida. He had read *When I Lay My Isaac Down*, and the note said, "I feel strongly your son should make application for his case to be heard in front of the Florida Clemency Board in December." A burst of unexpected hope exploded in my heart. I thought, *Someone in a position of leadership in the state of Florida believes Jason is not a threat to society and doesn't need to be locked up for the rest of his life.* At that moment, I believed that God not only heard my prayers but was in the process of providing the path to an eventual positive resolution.

My mind was spinning as I recalled the many people we met over the past couple of years — influential people in and out of Florida government positions, who were able to connect us to others who could offer advice and tangible help. Gene and I often looked at each other and exclaimed, "Now, *that* was a divine appointment!" It happened repeatedly, and I wondered if perseverance had finally paid off. Was God at work on a new kind miracle?

Jason submitted an application for clemency. It usually takes three to five years for that paperwork to make it to the top of the pile of thousands of applications from other inmates who request that their cases be evaluated by the Florida Parole Commission.

After I responded to the Florida official and expressed doubt that clemency could be an option, this response came: "Many people don't understand that clemency doesn't always mean instant release of an inmate. The clemency process can result in a commutation of a sentence, which means setting an end-of-sentence date. In your son's case, with a conviction of first-degree murder, you would definitely not be looking at instant release. The most you could hope for would be to receive an eventual end-of-sentence date."

My hope soared. Because Jason committed his crime when he was in his mid-twenties, even if his sentence was commuted to twenty-five or thirty years, he would still walk in freedom in this lifetime if granted some sort of clemency.

Gene and I had more questions than answers, but we formed a plan of action. Specific steps had to be taken within the next four months.

1. Petitions needed to be signed by people who believed that Jason would not be a threat to society if he were ever released.

2. We needed to locate a minimum of three people of influence, particularly those in government, who would write a personal letter to the governor and the clemency board asking that Jason's case be fast-tracked.

3. Certified paperwork on his case from the clerk of the circuit and county courts had to be filed with Jason's application for clemency. (This was more challenging than we anticipated because of how slowly paperwork is duplicated and mailed from many government offices.)

4. Letters of support for Jason needed to be written and delivered to the clemency board from people who knew our son before and/or after his arrest. The letters needed to voice confidence in his character and include the assurance that Jason had a strong network of family and friends who would assist him upon release. Most of all, the letters needed to assure the clemency board that Jason would not be a threat to society in the future.

The assignment was daunting — too time intensive for our busy ministry travel schedule — but that was not going to stop us. With much prayer and high energy, we began the process, one e-mail, phone call, and letter at a time. As a mom, I wished that Jason didn't need to be informed. I worried about getting his hopes up once again, only to have them toppled into ruins.

THE *Four-Month* MARATHON

Every spare minute of our time was devoted to the dream of getting Jason's case heard at the December 2006 clemency hearing. Our Stretcher Bearers, the remarkable group of family members and friends who prayed for us and provided tangible encouragement to us through the months and years leading up to the trial, once again supported us through intensive prayer and by writing letters.

Radio stations heard about our need for signed petitions and put the word out on the airwaves. And the mail started rolling in. Hundreds of people signed petitions, and almost one hundred letters came from government officials, Jason's fellow Naval Academy graduates, teachers, pastors, family members, and others who had connections with Jason during every stage of his growing-up years as well as from people who got to know him during his years of incarceration.

Three of those letters were uniquely special. The first was from my father:

My Dear Fellow Americans,

My name is Clyde Afman, age 83, World War II veteran, European theater, 13th Armored Division, recipient of the bronze star. My wife, Pauline, and I have been married for 60 years and we have raised six children. . . . I have been a pastor for the past 46 years. . . .

Our first child, Carol Joy, has but one child, a son, Jason Paul Kent . . . who has always been a high achiever and a compassionate man who loves God and his family. From early on he seemed destined for the military. He loved the Navy and took pride in serving his country as a naval officer. Then tragedy struck.

You good and discerning people have a difficult responsibility to decipher truth from error. . . . I plead for your mercy and compassion on behalf of a young man who has so much to give, who has an outstanding support base, and who could make a tremendous contribution to his fellow man and to his country if given the opportunity. . . . My prayer for him is that his life will not be wasted behind bars but that one day (perhaps soon) he will be free to make a great investment in his family and in society. . . . Thank you for considering this correspondence from an old man and a grandfather.

God Bless You,

Clyde Afman[3]

This letter of support from his grandfather was one of J.P.'s favorites. It was still hard for us to get used to our new kind of normal. There had been much pomp and pride as parents of a U.S. Naval Academy graduate, and now we spent our at-home weekends inside the razor wire of a maximum-security prison. Uniforms are worn in both places — but that is the only similarity.

Two letters arrived from friends of Jason, from both sides of the wall that separates our son from freedom. The first was from his former roommate, Captain Chad Van Someren, U.S. Marines. Chad's letter was on official Marine Corps stationery.

> Dear Governor Bush,
>
> If ever there was a time for clemency, this time is now.
>
> Jason Paul Kent has been justly sentenced for his crime. His sense of duty and obligation as a father to protect his family overwhelmed his normally good judgment. His crime was serious. His punishment is just.
>
> Why clemency?
>
> First, because Jason's guilt and remorse are real. He understands both the gravity of his crime and justice of his sentence.
>
> Second, because Jason's conduct in prison has demonstrated a character of exemplary integrity. His positive outlook, his profitable use of time, his increased maturity (moral, intellectual, and emotional) reveal a man determined to make positive contributions to society.
>
> Third, because Jason's positive contributions to society could be exponentially larger if he were free. This experience has been a defining experience for Jason. Far from being a threat to society, Jason's remorse is a springboard for a life dedicated to service; a rehabilitation of others, as he himself has been rehabilitated; a life dedicated to hope and second chances; a life characterized by both justice and mercy.
>
> When used wisely, clemency is profoundly beautiful and good. It takes into account character and compassion without minimizing the crime. I shared a room with Jason for four years at the Naval Academy and respect him as a man of courage, character, and sincerity. I've visited him in prison and have kept in touch through letters. His remorse is real, his conduct is exemplary, and his future is bright.

Thank you for your consideration!

Semper Fidelis,

Chad Van Someren

Captain, U.S. Marines[4]

The next letter came from Patrick, a man who was in prison with Jason. It was handwritten on notebook paper from the prison commissary.

To Whom It May Concern:

I met Jason Kent while incarcerated with him at Hardee Correctional Institution. As a veteran of the U.S. military, having served six years in the Navy, I was drawn to his natural leadership. Jason demonstrates daily the characteristics of an excellent leader and shows concern and compassion for other inmates.

Jason has been a strong Christian role model for me and for many others. When approached by other inmates who have personal, family, or court-related problems, Jason is quick to offer to pray with them. He rarely misses an opportunity to testify and evangelize. He selflessly offers his time to help other inmates with legal issues and with family-related struggles. . . .

Jason has shared with me his desire to help inmates through opening a halfway house and a program designed to help convicted felons who are leaving prison to continue on the right path and to ensure they have the education, tools, and resources they need to remain out of prison. . . . With the staggering number of inmates soon to be released from prisons . . . it is imperative that Jason Kent be granted clemency so he can begin to give back to society and help others in a way that few have the natural talent to do.

Sincerely,

Patrick McCrosky

Inmate, Hardee Correctional Institution

Bowling Green, FL[5]

WAITING *with* HOPE

Jason was deeply moved by the multiple letters of support. One day he said, "I feel like I'm reading my own obituary. Can you believe how gracious and kind people have been? I'm surprised they still remember me." During this time, our faith was bolstered. God reminded us of some key facts:

- People were still supportive, even though seven years had gone by since the murder.
- Most of the people who wrote didn't feel justice was served when Jason receive a life sentence without the possibility of parole.
- God was still at work in surprising and powerful ways. We were not forgotten.

We continued waiting. Then a call came from the governor's office. The caller identified herself as legal counsel to then Governor Jeb Bush. She was polite but firm. "I have discussed your request with the governor, and Jason's case will not be fast-tracked because he is not desperately ill and has not been incarcerated for a prolonged period of time." My mind whirled as my heart sank, and I had trouble verbalizing. Before hanging up, she said, "Your son's case will be in the system, and it will eventually rise to the top, but of course that will be under another administration, because Governor Bush will be leaving office at the end of December." Her voice softened, empathizing with our pain, and she continued, "Jason Kent has the best advocates any inmate could ever ask for. You have a wonderful family." And she hung up.

I felt ill. The disappointment was bitter. I wept uncontrollably.

VACILLATING *Emotions*

After believing I had laid my Isaac down, I found myself picking my Isaac (my hopes and dreams for my son) up again. Thousands of people had listened to me speak about letting go of my expectations about what our family reunions would look like, with Jason and his family around our Thanksgiving table and gathered around our Christmas tree. The people who read my book told me they found fresh hope and renewed faith in my example of what it means to discover the power of relinquishment. I felt like a failure as this recent experience reminded me that I wasn't all that good at letting go of my dream of a positive outcome for my son.

Then I did what I should have done earlier: I opened my Bible to see what God's Word says about perseverance and waiting. What I discovered reminded me that I was not the only person to experience disappointment with God. I especially identified with the psalmist:

- "I am exhausted from crying for help; my throat is parched. My eyes are swollen with weeping, waiting for my God to help me." (Psalm 69:3, NLT)
- "I am worn out waiting for your rescue, but I have put my hope in your word." (119:81, NLT)
- "LORD, I wait for you; you will answer, Lord my God." (38:15, NIV)

I really connected with the passage that talks about waiting for God to help me while my eyes are swollen from crying, and there was something very personal about Psalm 119:81 that gave me permission to say out loud, "God, I am *worn out* waiting for Your rescue!" I didn't feel like praying or talking or getting back to work on Jason's case. I felt like quitting.

THE *Unexpected* CALL

Months passed. Jeb Bush left office, and Charlie Crist became our new governor in the state of Florida. He had been the attorney general, and one of his campaign promises was to be tough on crime.

One afternoon a call came from our attorney. He said, "Gene and Carol, Jason's clemency application finally came to the top of the pile, and I've just received word that the Florida Parole Commission has recommended that his case be heard at the next clemency hearing." I was stunned. To my knowledge, we had no advocate in the office of the current administration, and this was a surprise beyond description. He continued, "In order to get that hearing, Jason has to be granted a waiver by the clemency aides (the attorneys and other professionals) who work for the four members of the clemency board: the governor, the attorney general, the head of the Department of Agriculture, and the chief financial officer. Both you and Gene will need to come to Tallahassee to present the case and request the waiver."

My heart was racing. We had been turned down so quickly by the previous administration. Was it possible that God's timing was different from what we expected earlier and He was still preparing a positive outcome for J.P.?

The date came, and we drove the four and a half hours to the state capital. After arriving at the building where the waiver hearing was to take place, we were handed a piece of paper with five cases listed. We were number three. At the top, it stated that we would have five minutes to present our case. Anxiety mounted. *Five minutes? How could it be possible to present the facts of such a huge case in five minutes?* We were allowed to observe as the first two cases were presented. I glanced at my watch. Each of them got fifteen minutes. Perhaps we would too.

It was our turn. My stomach twisted in knots as I took my seat next to Gene and our attorney. We had a desk in front of us, and all eight of the clemency aides were several steps above us, so they could look down on us from a higher vantage point. It was intimidating, frightening, nerve-racking.

Our attorney made some opening comments, briefly reviewing what the case was about, and then said, "Carol, why don't you begin and share what Jason was like in his growing-up years, along with your understanding of what happened and why you believe he should be given an opportunity for his case to be heard."

I gulped. My many years of public speaking had not prepared me for what felt like the most important speech of my life. I could hear a tremor in my voice as I began to talk about my son. The clemency aides leaned forward, listening intently and asking appropriate questions. Ten minutes into my presentation, I sensed the power of the Holy Spirit in that room. My fear was lessening, and God give me the courage to respond to the queries from this powerful group of government aides. Then Gene was asked to speak, followed by more questions: *Are there inmates and family members of inmates who would be willing to write letters in support of your son's work in the prison as an educator, mentor, and positive example? Are there jail and prison volunteers who've gotten to know Jason who would write letters on his behalf? Are there people who have known him before and after his incarceration who would vouch for his character?* We answered with an enthusiastic "Yes!"

As the panel began wrapping up our case, they asked us to gather these letters and submit them so that a decision could be made. I looked at my watch. One hour had passed since the panel had begun listening to our case. Our attorney told us that in the history of his work on clemency cases, he had never before seen the panel give that much time to a case at a waiver hearing. Gene and I both sensed the favor of God, and we returned home to begin collecting the requested letters.

It took two months for all of the letters to be gathered, along with DVDs of television programs that had been aired on Jason's case. We worked feverishly on this project. One inmate wrote, "I was nothing but a no-good addict before coming to prison, and Jason Kent led me to Jesus Christ." Some of the letters brought me to tears. Clearly, Jason was making a huge difference in the lives of many inmates.

When we finished this task, we put together eight identical notebooks for the clemency aides filled with powerful letters of support. Before shipping them to Tallahassee, we placed them in a box and prayed over the contents that had been gathered with time, love, and care. We prayed that God would use the letters to reveal Jason's true character to those who would evaluate whether or not he would receive a clemency hearing.

Three days later the phone rang. Our attorney said, "I'm sorry to tell you that I've received a form letter from the attorney to the governor, and it's stamped, 'Denied.' Jason will not receive a clemency hearing."

I fell into Gene's arms as he hung up the phone. We had worked and prayed so hard, and there hadn't been time for eight people in the four executive offices to read those notebooks and have a meeting to decide what to do. Jason's case had been given a rubber-stamp denial from the governor's office. It felt like a ridiculous farce that we had even been asked to collect the letters. I was tired of feeling like I'd been kicked in the gut. We knew by law that Jason would have to wait five years to fill out another application for clemency, and it would take another three to five years after that for his paperwork to once again rise to the top of the pile — a hopeless process.

A PICTURE *of* PERSEVERANCE

The next day was a visitation day. Because we're not allowed to make calls to our son, we would be telling him in person about what had happened. J.P. and a committed group of Christian inmate brothers had been fasting and praying on his behalf. I knew this news would be a bitter disappointment.

I was so upset I told Gene I couldn't go with him to the prison in the morning to tell Jason the result. I would come at noon. I was weeping as I finally walked through the second heavy metal door. Jason was waiting for me on the other side. I sobbed into his shoulder. Choking back the tears, I said, "I'm sorry, son. So much work has been done and we've prayed so hard. My heart aches for you and your brothers in Christ inside the prison who have fasted and prayed so fervently."

Looking up, I saw the peace of Jesus on Jason's face. Quietly, he said, "Mom, if we were given the waiver and my case was scheduled for a clemency hearing, we might have thought it was because we had the best attorney, or we might have thought it was because we had the favor of politicians." He paused, and with a humble spirit, he continued. "The way this has happened, we know the only way I'll ever walk in freedom again in this lifetime is when God says I've served enough time and I can help Him more outside the razor wire than I can on the inside. And if that never happens on this earth, we need to realize life is short and we'll all walk in freedom in heaven very soon."

That day my son consoled me and I came to understand Romans 5:2-5 in a personal and penetrating way:

We boast in the hope of the glory of God. Not only so, but we also glory in our sufferings, because we know that suffering produces perseverance; perseverance, character; and character, hope. And hope does not put us to shame, because God's love has been poured out into our hearts through the the Holy Spirit, who has been given to us. (NIV)

Jason understood the power of perseverance — the kind of "waiting with hope" that it not defined by the immediate results I was praying for.

The HOMECOMING

For so many years, April faithfully took Chelsea and Hannah to visit Jason. Then came the hurricanes of 2004. Three of those horrific storms went right through the center of the state, directly through Lake Wales, where April lived. The storms caused major damage to her home. The roof leaked, wallboard warped, and mold started growing in the carpet, closets, and drawers. I sensed something in April's spirit break during the months of cleanup that followed.

A year later she came to us and said, "I've decided to move out of state with the girls, and if I separate from J.P., I will no longer be in touch with the two of you." Gene and I had great compassion for all she had been through, and although our hearts were breaking, we understood her desire to move away from the place where she'd known great pain. With heavy hearts, we said good-bye to April and the girls. Chelsea was twelve and Hannah was nine.

It was hard for me to keep bitterness at bay because my precious step-granddaughters were being taken out of our lives. Over the next few years, as birthdays and Christmases came and went, we sent gifts and cards but never knew if they were received.

Six and a half years went by. It was August of 2011, and I was attending a Bible-software training seminar with my friend and fellow speaker Kendra Smiley. One afternoon we had a few private moments together, and she asked about our son and his family. I shared with her that the girls were now nineteen and sixteen, and I wondered how long we should keep sending gifts to them when we never knew if they were received or not. I smiled and said, "I don't want to be a stalker grandmother if they'd rather not have me in their lives."

Without a moment's hesitation, Kendra replied, "Carol, don't ever stop. As long as the gifts are not refused, those girls will always know that you and Gene love them." I thanked her for her helpful advice.

One month later, I was speaking at Malone University in Canton, Ohio.

On the trip home, Gene and I had a layover in Atlanta. I was going to spend a few days there with girlfriends, and Gene was heading home to Florida. He and I had lunch together at the airport and said our good-byes. A half hour passed. When we're away, our home phone is forwarded to Gene's cell phone.

Gene and I were both still in the airport but far from each other. My cell phone rang. Gene was breathless as he said, "Carol, I just got off the phone with Chelsea." He said, "A soft voice said, 'Grampy, it's Chelsea. I'm nineteen years old and I'm a freshman in college. And I miss my family.'"

Tears of joy flowed freely that day. Chelsea came to our home for Thanksgiving weekend and had a reunion with her dad. She spent her month-long Christmas vacation with us and came for the week of spring break two months later. Hannah graduated from high school the following May and asked if she, along with Chelsea, could spend the summer at our house.

It is impossible to describe the range of emotions we've experienced as we've gotten reacquainted with the girls and as Jason has had a chance to get to know his stepdaughters as young adults. We marvel at the way God answered our prayers for them and at the miraculous way they've come back into our lives.

At this writing, Jason and April are still married, but they are separated and we don't know what the end of this story will be. We love her and want to respect the privacy she desires. Those of you who have incarcerated loved ones know how difficult life is for the family members, and we know that what Jason's wife has gone through is unspeakably hard and deeply emotionally painful. We ache for her losses on multiple levels, and we continue to mourn for the family of the deceased.

Both Chelsea and Hannah are busy college students, and we're very proud of them and thrilled for the laughter, joy, and energy they bring into our lives. During the six years of their absence, Jason wrote to them often, even over the many years he heard nothing from them, and he's enjoying the opportunity of giving them encouragement and advice now. In retrospect, we understand that at times, when we pray in faith believing for a positive outcome to the deep-seated requests of our hearts, it feels as though God isn't listening and that no one really cares about our needs. For me, when I didn't get the "big" answer to my prayers (an eventual end-of-sentence date for my son), it was hard to focus on the many ways in which God was powerfully at work.

Having the girls back in our lives has reminded us that perseverance is more important than we ever imagined. It took steadfastness to keep being intentional about sending notes and gifts, whether or not they were received, and we now know how much the girls looked forward to hearing from us even though they were not allowed to contact us.

WHAT IS JASON *Doing* NOW?

I've watched perseverance in action as my son focuses on encouraging and mentoring fellow inmates, knowing that purpose in life is not determined by how much money we make or where we live. All of Jason's belongings must fit in a small 1 x 1½ foot steel lockbox or they will be confiscated or stolen. Those possessions include legal papers, letters from loved ones, pictures of family members, canteen items, books he's reading, and his Bible.

J.P. has reminded me, "With all my heart, I long for the 'burden' of a job, the challenge of house and car payments, and the joy of being with my family — loving them and providing for them. But I have also learned while being in prison that I don't need a lot of 'things' to make me happy. That part of this unwanted experience has been useful, and it has helped keep me on course as I live day by day in a hard place."

Perseverance for Jason involves taking one day at a time instead of dwelling on having no hope of life outside the prison walls. For him, focusing on doing one thing every day to help a fellow inmate hold on to faith or using his gift of leadership to facilitate a class or help resolve a conflict on the compound brings J.P. closer to eternity. He writes,

> Joy, for me, is knowing as concretely as I know my name and my
> birthday that God is real and that He loves me personally and that I'm
> never alone and He can be trusted with my heart.
>
> How I wish that pain of this magnitude didn't accompany my

personal growth, especially the suffering of my victim's family and my own family.

I'm discovering that any joy in the midst of this horrendous ordeal is a surprising gift from God. Mom, I desire for all of us healing and rest. I pray that your heart will smile.[6]

Jason has taken more than five hundred inmates through Dave Ramsey's Financial Peace University course, teaching them how to develop a budget and balance a checkbook. He's led biblical-counseling classes, instructing men in how to be good husbands and fathers. He also meets with his workout buddies and prayer team and is using his leadership skills to mentor the inmates around him.

SPEAK UP *for* HOPE

Ministry opportunities multiplied as we began to openly share our story. It's been a privilege to speak at Women of Faith, Extraordinary Women, and Women of Joy events as well as for conferences and retreats all over the country, reminding people to make hope-filled choices based on God's eternal truth. Gene and I often speak at Sunday-morning worship services together, and he shares about the tears of a father and the purposeful actions we can take when we use what's happened in our lives as a platform upon which we can give others fresh faith and courage.

We launched the nonprofit organization Speak Up for Hope, and we have been privileged to place DVD teaching series, books, and Bibles in prison chapels in many states. We regularly fill Boxes of Hope for wives and moms of inmates, and we collect games, coloring books, and crayons for the prison visitation areas so children have something to do with their incarcerated parents during their visits.

God has reminded us that we need to look around and see who needs help and lift a hand to offer others personal encouragement and tangible support. Proverbs 31:8-9 speaks deeply to us:

Speak up for the people who have no voice,
> for the rights of all the down-and-outers.
Speak out for justice!
> Stand up for the poor and destitute!

If you would like to stand with us as we persevere as long as God invites us to join Him on this journey, please contact us at SpeakUpforHope.org.

Hebrews 12:1-3 is an encouraging reminder of the power of perseverance:

Do you see what this means — all these pioneers who blazed the way, all these veterans cheering us on? It means we'd better get on with it. Strip down, start running — and never quit! No extra spiritual fat, no parasitic sins. Keep your eyes on _Jesus_, who both began and finished this race we're in. Study how he did it. Because he never lost sight of where he was headed — that exhilarating finish in and with God — he could put up with anything along the way: Cross, shame, whatever. And now he's _there_, in the place of honor, right alongside God. When you find yourselves flagging in your faith, go over that story again, item by item, that long litany of hostility he plowed through. _That_ will shoot adrenaline into your souls!

THE CHURCH _of the_ RAZOR WIRE

Gene and I moved to Florida eight years ago in order to be closer to our son and to support what he is doing in ministry on the prison compound. Friends ask, "Where do you go to church now that you moved to Florida?" We tell them, "We go to the Church of the Razor Wire."

They raise an eyebrow and ask, "What denomination is _that_?" We let them know that Saturdays and Sundays are visitation days at the prisons in Florida and we're usually somewhere else in the country on most Saturdays at speaking engagements. We often take the last flight home on Saturday night or the first flight on Sunday morning so we can have our private church service at our table in the visitation area. And when we can't get back in time, friends and relatives visit J.P. in our absence.

Last fall I was invited to speak to the inmates at Hardee Correctional Institution, where J.P. resides. The men were enthusiastic and respectful as I shared our journey of receiving a middle-of-the-night phone call that forever changed our lives. Several prison officials joined us, and they, too, listened carefully to my message.

I told the inmates that statistics tell us only 6 percent of them had loving fathers, and my heart aches for all they have experienced. But I reminded them that they can be the first person in their family to change the future generations. I began to hear the sound of weeping. At the end, I challenged the men to be intentional about four things:

1. Know Jesus personally.
2. Write out a gratitude list of everything you have to be thankful for.
3. Write to your children, even if you never hear from them.
4. Do one act of kindness for someone on the prison compound every day.

As I prayed over the inmates, grown men were weeping and some were sobbing. The Spirit of the Lord was in that place.

For me, laying my Isaac down is a daily choice to say, "God, not my will but Thine be done. Help me not to waste this unexpected opportunity to serve You by saying yes when you open doors to share my story, weep with those who weep, and rejoice with those who are celebrating. Help me to focus, with perseverance, on continuing in a state of grace that finally leads to a state of glory."

God's Power in *Your* Circumstances

Living through the past decade has reminded me of the truth found in this quotation by Walter Elliot: "Perseverance is not a long race; it is many short races one after the other."[7] There are times in our lives when we think it will be impossible to survive an unthinkable crisis. But somehow we keep breathing and we continue doing "the next thing." Eventually, we realize we have made it through an entire day, then a full week, and sometimes we're startled when we are still functioning a month later. In our case, the months have now become years, and one thing is certain: Our faith remains unshakable when we press into God's truth and keep putting one foot in front of the other as we conquer "one short race after another."

Sometimes I don't like the process. James says, "Consider it pure joy, my brothers and sisters, whenever you face trials of many kinds, because you know that the testing of your faith produces perseverance. Let perseverance finish its work so that you may be mature and complete, not lacking anything" (James 1:2-4, NIV). I'm still working on that challenging paradox of choosing joy when I face trials, but I've traveled this journey long enough to know that the testing of my faith does indeed develop perseverance. Unshakable faith in unthinkable circumstances is possible when we persevere and experience a state of grace that leads us to a state of glory. I'm not good at that every day. But one short race after another gets me closer to eternal glory, and that reality motivates me!

1. Has there been a time in your life when, on the surface, it seemed that God did not answer your prayer? Did you come to a place where you could see His hand at work in other ways and were you able to recognize His presence in your situation?

2. On a scale of 1 to 10 (with 10 being high), how good are you at perseverance when the outcome of a personal challenge doesn't have a desired outcome? How does your response impact your faith?

3. During the past five years when my father (in his late eighties) would leave a visit with Jason, he repeatedly said, "That boy is not just surviving, he's thriving as he lives for the Lord in this unlikely place." My dad left for heaven last year before his prayer for Jason to walk in freedom came to pass, but he realized the benefits of Jason's perseverance in the middle of unthinkable circumstances. What benefits have you experienced when you waited on God for a miracle?

4. I wrote about how I identified with the words of the psalmist in Psalm 119:8: "I am worn out waiting for your rescue, but I have put my hope in your word" (NLT). What verses from God's Word have

helped you focus on hope when life is turning out differently than your expectations?

5. This book began with a quotation from Eric Liddell, the Olympian: "Circumstances may appear to wreck our lives and God's plans, but God is not helpless among the ruins." How have you experienced the truth of that statement?

6. What is the most significant "takeaway" challenge from this book that will help you choose unshakable faith in unthinkable circumstances?

$\mathcal{A}$CKNOWLEDGMENTS

I AM INDEBTED TO MY DEAR FRIEND BONNIE KEEN, FOR inspiring the title of this book. We shared the platform at a women's conference, and when she sang her signature song, "Isaac," my spirit was quickened and I knew the age-old story of Abraham and Isaac represented what God was asking me to do — not just to let go of my control over my circumstances and the outcome of my son's trial, but to be vulnerable enough to tell our story.

It is in being real by telling our stories that we give other people permission to be open and honest about their own lives. All pretense dissolves and we begin to share at a heart level. Music speaks to the soul when we are in too much pain to read or to think. In the middle of my struggle, the right music always triggers healthy tears and flows over me with healing reminders of timeless truth. Bonnie, thank you for your permission to title this book *When I Lay My Isaac Down*. (If you are in a hard place, Bonnie Keen's CDs, *Marked for Life* and *God of Many Chances*, will breathe fresh faith into your aching soul. See www.BonnieKeen.com.)

On a writing project that forced me to relive horrific circumstances and review journals and news clippings of deep sadness and personal trauma, I had to have an editor who was first a longtime friend, and second, the best developmental editor in the country. That person is Traci Mullins of Eclipse Editorial Services. Traci, you poured your heart and soul into this project and demanded personal authenticity, profound honesty, and gut-wrenching accuracy. Thank you for holding me to a high standard of excellence and for feeling with me every ounce of emotion you asked me to relive. My respect for the quality of your work is off the charts. My love for you as a friend is immense. You formed the shape of this manuscript and turned the words of my heart into something I pray will encourage others to find faith, hope, and joy in the middle of their own challenging circumstances.

This book is filled with the true stories of people who have endured unthinkable circumstances. Due to the personal nature of the stories and the need to protect the privacy of the individuals involved, I am not able to list your names here, but you know who you are. Because of your honesty, readers will know that they, too, can find purpose, meaning, and a future even if their "Isaac experience" seems unbearable. I salute your bravery, your honesty, and your willingness to help others through telling your stories. My life is richer for the friendship we share.

I wish I could design a flag and wave it from the rooftop to acknowledge our remarkable family and friends who have stood by our side and held us up when we were too weak to stand and in too much pain to pray for ourselves. My family, Gene's family, and our Stretcher Bearers have "been there" for us night and day and we love you! Kathy Blume, Kathe Wunnenberg, and Becky Freeman kept our prayer requests and tangible needs communicated to those who stood in the gap for us. Thank you for your selfless commitment to this task!

Shirley Liechty and Laurie Dennis, our administrative assistants at Speak Up Speaker Services, fielded calls, responded to reporters, cared for the ongoing demands in our office, and offered daily personal encouragement. Cathy Gallagher did hours of research on key principles featured in this book. Jan Fleck, lifelong friend and encourager, made herself available whenever she was needed. I am also grateful for the research of Jackie Kendall, a gifted Bible teacher and extraordinary communicator, for contributing the powerful teaching on "the Ephraim blessing." Jackie, you have reminded me to be "fruitful in suffering." (For additional information, go to www.JackieKendall.com.)

To work with a publishing house that believes in publishing books that enable me to be more effective in communicating my message is a gift beyond description. I am grateful to publisher Dan Rich and editorial director Terry Behimer for providing a day of brainstorming at NavPress headquarters with your *best* editorial team. Thank you for believing in my potential and for standing by me throughout the process of working on this manuscript. Your creativity, vision, and passion for producing great books inspire me! I am also grateful to Karen Lee-Thorp for her significant contribution to the early formation stage of this book.

Finally, this book could not have been written without my husband, Gene Kent. He opened his journals, his heart, and his painful memories, and then freed me to write the truth of our experience. He was there when I had to pause in my writing because of fresh tears. He continues to be my comforter, my encourager, my partner, and my inspiration. No one could have a better husband or father than you, Gene. I love you!

$\mathcal{N}$OTES

PROLOGUE
1. Anne Lamott, *Traveling Mercies: Some Thoughts on Faith* (New York: Pantheon, 1999), p. 49.

CHAPTER 1
1. James 1:5-6, MSG.
2. Genesis 28:16, NIV.
3. John 6:60, MSG.
4. John 6:67, MSG.
5. John 6:68-69, MSG.

CHAPTER 2
1. Henry Pierson Curtis, *The Orlando Sentinel*, November 6, 1999, p. 1.
2. Genesis 22:1-17, MSG.
3. Larry Richards, *Every Man in the Bible* (Nashville, Tenn.: Thomas Nelson, 1999), p. 20.
4. Genesis 12:1-3, NIV, italics mine.
5. Lysa TerKeurst, *Radically Obedient, Radically Blessed*, (Eugene, Ore.: Harvest House, 2003), p. 37.
6. *Merriam-Webster's Collegiate Dictionary*, 10th ed., s.v. "Sacrifice."
7. Psalm 116:1-6, MSG.
8. *Webster's New World Dictionary of the American Language*, s.v. "Relinquish," p. 841.
9. John 12:24, MSG.

CHAPTER 3

1. John 11:35, NIV.

2. John 11:21, MSG.

3. John 11:32, MSG.

4. John 11:37, MSG, italics mine.

5. John 11:33, MSG, italics mine.

6. John 11:38, MSG, italics mine.

7. John 11:39, MSG.

8. John 11:39, MSG.

9. John 11:40, MSG.

10. John 11:41, MSG.

11. John 11:43, MSG.

12. John 11:44, MSG.

13. John 11:35, NIV.

14. Psalm 126:5-6, NIV.

15. Psalm 56:8, MSG.

16. Ken Gire, *Windows of the Soul* (Grand Rapids, Mich.: Zondervan, 1996), p. 194.

17. Psalm 34:18, NIV.

18. Psalm 91:1-2,14-16, MSG.

19. Psalm 51:17, MSG.

20. Revelation 7:17, MSG.

CHAPTER 4

1. Michael Slater, *Becoming a Stretcher Bearer* (Ventura, CA: Regal Books, 1985). Formerly published under the title, *Stretcher Bearers*. Stretcher Bearer Ministries, P.O. Box 1035, La Habra, CA, 90633-1035. or 562.943.7676.

2. Luke 5:17-26, MSG.

3. Galatians 6:2, NIV.

4. Jess Moody, quoted by Lloyd Cory, *Quotable Quotes* (Wheaton, Ill.: Victor, 1985), p. 76.

5. Philippians 2:1-4, MSG.

6. Romans 12:13, MSG.

7. *Alcoholics Anonymous*, Third edition, 1976, p. 151.

8. *Alcoholics Anonymous*, Third edition, 1976, p. 64.

9. Karen Burton Mains, *Comforting One Another* (Nashville, Tenn.: Thomas Nelson, 1997), pp. 119-120.

10. Romans 15:1-7, MSG.

CHAPTER 5

1. Lisa Beamer, with Ken Abraham, *Let's Roll* (Wheaton, Ill.: Tyndale, 2002), p. 296.

2. Gracia Burnham, with Dean Merrill, *In the Presence of My Enemies* (Wheaton, Ill.: Tyndale, 2003), p. 307.

3. *Merriam-Webster's Collegiate Dictionary*, 10th ed., s.v. "Hope (v.)."

4. *Merriam-Webster's Collegiate Dictionary*, 10th ed., s.v. "Hope (n.)."

5. Proverbs 13:12, NLT.

6. Psalm 27:13-14, NASB.

7. Gabriel Marcel, quoted by Dan Allender, *The Healing Path* (Colorado Springs, Colo.: WaterBrook, 1999), p. 78.

8. Psalm 62:5-7, NLT.

9. Isaiah 40:31, NIV.

10. Romans 4:18-22, NIV.

11. Henry Blackaby, *Created to Be God's Friend: How God Shapes Those He Loves* (Nashville, Tenn.: Thomas Nelson, 1999), pp. 70-71.

12. Hebrews 6:19, NIV.

13. Gregory Floyd, *A Grief Unveiled*, quoted by Nancy Guthrie, *Holding on to Hope*, (Wheaton, Ill.: Tyndale, 2002), p. x.

CHAPTER 6

1. Jim Cymbala, with Dean Merrill, *Fresh Faith: What Happens When Real Faith Ignites God's People* (Grand Rapids, Mich.: Zondervan, 1999), p. 11.

2. *Great Is Thy Faithfulness* (Carol Stream, Ill.: Hope Publishing, 1923).

3. Max Lucado, *Grace for the Moment* (Nashville, Tenn.: J. Countryman, 2000), p. 248.

4. John 5:1-9.

5. Hebrews 11:1, NIV.

6. John 5:8, NIV.

7. See Psalm 61:2, NIV.

8. Deuteronomy 33:27, NIV.

9. Oswald Chambers, *My Utmost for His Highest: An Updated Edition in Today's Language*, ed. James Reimann, (Grand Rapids, Mich.: Discovery House, 1992), March 19 entry.

10. Cymbala, *Fresh Faith*, pp. 93-94.

11. Genesis 22:6, NIV.

12. Genesis 22:6-7, NIV.

13. Genesis 22:7, NIV.

14. Genesis 22:7, NIV.

15. Genesis 22:8, NIV.

16. Hebrews 11:17-19, MSG.

17. Genesis 22:9-14, NIV.

18. Hebrews 11:32-40, MSG.

19. Henry Blackaby, *Created to Be God's Friend: How God Shapes Those He Loves* (Nashville, Tenn.: Thomas Nelson, 1999), pp. 70-71.

20. Ralph Waldo Emerson, *Essays: First Series (1841), Essay IV—Spiritual Laws*.

21. Hebrews 11:1, MSG, italics mine.

CHAPTER 7

1. *Merriam-Webster's Collegiate Dictionary*, 10th ed., s.v. "Wait."

2. Philippians 4:6-7, TLB.

3. Psalm 91:4, NIV.

4. Psalm 30:5, NLT.

5. *New Webster's Dictionary and Thesaurus*, s.v. "Joy."

6. 1 Thessalonians 4:13.

7. Hebrews 12:2, NLT, italics mine.

8. Matthew 28:6-7, MSG.

9. Larry Crabb, *Shattered Dreams* (Colorado Springs, Colo.: WaterBrook, 2001), pp. 4, 198.

10. Galatians 6:2, NIV.

11. Hebrews 12:2, NIV.

12. Michael Card, *A Violent Grace* (Sisters, Ore.: Multnomah, 2000), p. 75.

13. Henri Nouwen, "Take This Cup" from *Can You Drink the Cup?* (Notre Dame, Ind.: Ave Maria Press, 1996).

CHAPTER 8
1. Genesis 18:25, KJV.

2. Jim Cymbala, with Dean Merrill, *Fresh Wind, Fresh Fire* (Grand Rapids, Mich.: Zondervan, 1997), p. 19.

3. Oswald Chambers, *My Utmost for His Highest: An Updated Edition in Today's Language* ed. James Reimann, (Grand Rapids, Mich.: Discovery House, 1992), July 28 entry.

4. John 12:26-28, MSG.

5. Leslie Williams, *Night Wrestling* (Dallas, Tex.: Word, 1997), p. 1.

6. Genesis 32:26, NIV.

7. Proverbs 31:8-9, MSG.

8. Isaiah 61:3, KJV.

9. Isaiah 45:3, NLT.

10. Gary Thomas, *Authentic Faith* (Grand Rapids, Mich.: Zondervan, 2002), p. 45.

11. Rick Warren, *The Purpose Driven Life* (Grand Rapids, Mich.: Zondervan, 2002), p. 290.

12. Frederick Buechner, quoted by Tim Hansel, *You Gotta Keep Dancin'* (Elgin, Ill.: David C. Cook, 1985), p. 19.

13. Genesis 41:52, NIV.

14. Genesis 41:51, NIV.

15. 1 Peter 1:4-9 MSG.

EPILOGUE
1. Richard Alves, quoted in Billy Grammer, *Perspectives on Pursuing Bold Love* (Dallas: Fellowship Bible Church Counseling Center, 1997), audio tape series.

2. Pastor Jim Cymbala.

3. Michael Yaconelli, *Messy Spirituality* (Grand Rapids, Mich.: Zondervan, 2002), p. 124.

EPILOGUE TO THE 2013 EDITION

1. Wordnik, s.v. "perseverance," accessed May 10, 2013, http://www.wordnik
.com/words/perseverance.

2. Carol Kent, *Between a Rock and a Grace Place* (Grand Rapids, MI: Zondervan,
2010), 26, 27, 29.

3. Carol Kent, *A New Kind of Normal* (Nashville: Thomas Nelson, 2007), 139–
140.

4. Kent, *Normal*, 141–142.

5. Kent, *Normal*, 142–143.

6. Kent, *Rock and a Grace Place*, 142–143.

7. Walter Elliot, http://www.brainyquote.com/quotes/keywords/perseverance
.html.

ABOUT THE AUTHOR

CAROL KENT is a popular international public speaker who is best known for being dynamic, humorous, encouraging, and biblical. She is a former radio-show cohost and has been a guest many times on *Focus on the Family* and a featured speaker at Women of Faith and Women of Joy arena events. She has also spoken at The Praise Gathering for Believers and at Vision New England's Congress and is a frequent speaker at Extraordinary Women events.

Carol has spoken internationally in South Africa, Germany, China, Korea, Hong Kong, Guatemala, Mexico, and Canada. She regularly appears on a wide variety of nationally syndicated radio and television broadcasts. Past appearances have included *Dateline NBC, CNN Live, The Billy Graham Television Special, "It Is Written" TV, Family Talk, On Main Street, LIFE Today with James Robison, Prime Time America, Midday Connection, Family Life Today,* and *100 Huntley Street.* Carol has also been a keynote speaker for the televised and nationally syndicated women's conference sponsored by Church Communications Network.

She is the president of Speak Up Speaker Services, a Christian speakers' bureau, and the founder and director of the Speak Up Conference, where she equips the next generation to speak, write, and lead. She founded the nonprofit organization Speak Up for Hope, which benefits the families of incarcerated individuals.

Carol holds a master's degree in communication arts and a bachelor's degree in speech education. She has taught speech and drama, and she has directed women's ministries at a large midwestern church. She is a member of the Advanced Writers and Speakers Association and serves on the advisory board of MOPS International.

Her books include *Between a Rock and a Grace Place*, *A New Kind of Normal*, *Miracle on Hope Hill* (cowritten with Jennie Afman Dimkoff), *When I Lay My Isaac Down*, *Becoming a Woman of Influence*, *Mothers Have Angel Wings*, *Secret Longings of the Heart*, *Tame Your Fears*, *Speak Up with Confidence*, and *Detours, Tow Trucks, and Angels in Disguise*. She also cowrote with Karen Lee-Thorp the DESIGNED FOR INFLUENCE Bible studies. Carol has been featured on the cover of *Today's Christian Woman*, and her articles have been published in a wide variety of magazines.

To schedule Carol to speak for your event, please contact:

Speak Up Speaker Services
586.481.7661
www.SpeakUpSpeakerServices.com
or
www.CarolKent.org

E-mail: Speakupinc@aol.com

For information on the Speak Up Conference,
go to SpeakUpConference.com.

For information on the ministry to inmates and their families,
go to SpeakUpforHope.org.

$\mathcal{S}$peak Up for Hope

is a nonprofit organization that seeks to
live out the principle of Proverbs 31:8-9, MSG:

"Speak up for the people who have no voice,
for the rights of all the down-and-outers.
Speak out for justice.
Stand up for the poor and destitute!"

To accomplish this mission, we will:

• Assist churches and organizations in adopting a prison to provide
hands-on encouragement to inmates and their families by working with the prison chaplain to supply needed assistance spiritually,
emotionally, and financially.

• Network educators with prison chaplains in order to provide GED
programs, marriage and family classes, vocational training, and college credit programs that will give purposeful living to prisoners.

• Cooperate with existing prison ministries that share our goals.

• Connect business professionals with soon-to-be-released inmates to
offer job opportunities that provide a chance for a fresh start.

• Provide funding for Speak Up With Confidence communications
training to mission and nonprofit organizations in the U.S. and abroad.

It is the goal of Speak Up for Hope to give hope to the hopeless, encouragement and strength to the weary, healing to marriages that have been torn

apart by incarceration, and mental, spiritual, and physical stability to the children of prisoners.

We pray that people all over the world will begin speaking up for those who cannot speak up for themselves. As people become the hands and feet of Jesus to "the least of these," something miraculous happens. As we choose to get personally involved by giving, volunteering, and praying, we are transformed from the inside out as we model for others how to become hope-givers.

Carol Kent

Carol Kent, Founder

Gene Kent

Gene Kent, Executive Director

For more information on the variety of ways in which you can be involved in Speak Up for Hope, please contact:

Speak Up for Hope
P.O. Box 6262
Lakeland, FL 33807
www.speakupforhope.org
888.987.1212

Please make tax deductible contributions payable to: Speak Up for Hope.

More Books from Best-Selling Author Carol Kent.

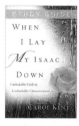

When I Lay My Isaac Down Study Guide

In the companion workbook to *When I Lay My Isaac Down*, you will see how Carol and Gene's personal story can bolster your faith, renew your hope, and challenge you to new levels of spiritual renewal. For individual or small-group study.

978-1-61291-452-7

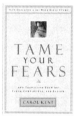

Tame Your Fears

Carol Kent examines ten fears common to most women and suggests ways to overcome such fears by using them as stepping stones to deeper faith, renewed confidence, and sincere reverence for God.

978-1-57683-359-9

Secret Longings of the Heart

Here is a rich encounter with the hidden desires of women today—the passions that determine lifestyle, behavior, and attitudes—and how these relate to your everyday life.

978-1-57683-360-5

To order copies, call NavPress at 1-800-366-7788 or log on to www.navpress.com.

Discipleship Inside Out*

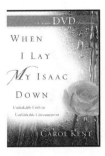

When I Lay My Isaac Down Curriculum DVD

8 Session DVD Curriculum Teaching Companion

The DVD teaching companion to the best-selling book *When I Lay My Isaac Down* comes with everything you need for facilitating life-changing small-group discussion or leading a soul-transforming retreat. It includes:

- A 2-DVD set of 8 powerful lessons such as:
  - *An Unexpected Journey: The Power of Unthinkable Circumstances*
  - *Why Didn't God Do Something?: The Power of Heartache*
  - *But Where Is the Lamb?: The Power of Faith*
  - *Embracing the Upside-Down Nature of the Cross: The Power of Joy*

- A 16-page, easy-to-use leader's guide, which includes lesson outlines and discussion starters
- Printable worksheets for participants (for women and couples)

Bonus features include:
  - Promotional clips, making publicity easy for your group!
  - A music video of the song "Isaac," featuring Bonnie Keen
  - Compelling testimonies of two other poignant Isaac stories
  - *A Father's Perspective:* A moving interview with Gene and Carol Kent for use with couples' groups

978-1-61291-453-4

To order copies, call NavPress at 1-800-366-7788 or
log on to www.navpress.com.

NAVPRESS

Discipleship Inside Out®